The Sixth Seal Signs

An Investigation of the Astronomical Signs in Revelation 6

Ender E. Law

For my A-Team,
my wife & children.
Thank you for all your love, patience,
collaboration and support.
"God's plan is coming together"

"People who can write intelligently about the Mazzaroth and the scriptures are very rare. I have only encountered half a dozen or less and I have consumed old books and blogs like one obsessed. You've stepped into some very exclusive shoes and it looks like they fit." Social Science Philosopher

"You've opened my eyes to the mysteries of Revelation. I did not realize so much of what is written in the Bible points to the constellations and it feels true in my heart. Thank you". Sheree B. Substack subscriber

"I love all the work you have done on Bible Prophecy. It totally blows my mind, especially your article on the corona virus. I can't wait to read your articles. Awesome work!" S. G. Substack subscriber

"That math is staggering. Our God does the impossible. Thank you for putting this together" Dr. Sherri Tenpenny, DO, AOBNMM, ABIHM

"I like the way you reason. Not shallow, shows thorough research, but also puts a challenge to the reader to read and comprehend (and apply). " Mary Foster, Agriculture Conservationist, retired

"It always takes me a long time to get through your articles, with all the links, charts and thinking through the analysis :-) but I so appreciate your work." njrsrie, Substack subscriber

"These books are fascinating! If you want to go deeper to understand the Bible, these books are a must. The Bible will come alive with current events and you will see just how accurate God's Word really is…you realize that only a Great God could set these things in motion from the beginning of time ("In the beginning…") and finish the end of the Bible with one word from Revelation…"Amen" (make it so)." Reviewer on Amazon

Books:

- *The Sixth Seal Signs* (2023, 2026)

- *The Covenant Signs* (2024)

- *The Signs of Jonah* (2025)

- *The Signs of the Four Horsemen* (2025)

Substack: https://ephesians610.substack.com/

- Over 250 articles

- More books being researched, brainstormed and drafted

Finally, be strong in the Lord

and in the strength of His might.

Ephesians 6:10, NASB1995

Table of Contents

Diagrams, Tables, and Timelines

Prologue

- Did the 2023 Earthquake in Turkey have biblical significance or was it like any other seismic event in history?

- What is the significance of three North American solar eclipses?

- What does the "sky split like a scroll" mean?

There are so many that recognize the significance of the times we live in. It motivates us to look deeper into God's Word for understanding of the Signs of the Times and to live the good news of Jesus Christ - to persevere in truth and strength without fear.

This is a ministry of love to all readers as we unpack the bible prophecies and prepare to look up, to be alert and watchful of the signs. Ephesians 6:10 is the beginning of one of the most important passages in equipping Christians to be spiritually battle-ready against forces of evil with the Full Armor of God which led me to writing on substack.

After prayer, study, and publishing over 200 articles on https://ephesians610.substack.com/ covering Revelation 12 the Great Heavenly signs, Revelation 13 Beasts, The Four Horsemen, Transhumanism, etc. the next logical step was to study Revelation 6, the sixth seal.

The research that has gone into *The Sixth Seal Signs* was first published online, between March 16th, 2023 to June 8th, 2023. Literally three months went by like a whirlwind and it was a fantastic journey of discovery. These articles have been organized into chapters for an end-to-end narrative, to improve readability, to provide additional research where appropriate, and archivability for posterity. The probability calculations are included immediately after each sign, thus grouping the chapters by sign.

There has been great division, death, deception, and darkness in the world since this journey began, yet these signs remind us to look up with hope, strength, and perseverance. The interpretations in this book are literal, scientifically researched, statistically analyzed, uplifting, and written to make the reader look up in wonder at the Heavens and to be watchful.

> The Heavens declare the glory of God, and the sky above proclaims his handiwork. Day to day pours out speech, and night to night reveals knowledge. Psalm 19:1–2, ESV[1]

This journey started with a curiosity in the Star of Bethlehem. What was this star that the Magi saw and why did it stop over Bethlehem? A few of these articles were published during the Christmas season on https://ephesians610.substack.com/ and more research is being drafted for a fifth book, *The Signs of Immanuel.*

Then the analysis led to the blood moons where some theologians believe these are possibly harbingers of things to come. The blood moons were followed by other interesting Heavenly signs, conjunctions of sun, moon, and planets with constellations. But what is the significance of the constellations and who named them? Orion and the Pleiades are mentioned in the book of Job, but how could this be? Did God name the stars and constellations before the flood?

Most noteworthy, the Revelation 12 great Heavenly signs (i.e.: The woman giving birth and the fiery red dragon), which some believe were fulfilled September 23rd, 2017.

The Revelation 12 sign was also preceded by a solar eclipse on August 21st, 2017. A solar eclipse that crossed North America passing over 7 Salems. What did this mean? Was this just coincidence? Was there more in the Heavenly wonders? Seven years later is another solar eclipse on April 8th, 2024.

The Sixth Seal series of articles led to researching and calculating the probability of these signs. This personal investigative study strengthened my faith and became a tremendous blessing. It quickly became mathematically impossible that these signs aligned with scripture coincidental. God is in total control of the Heavenly bodies.

---

[1] The Holy Bible: English Standard Version (Ps 19:1–2). (2016). Crossway Bibles.

In late 2025, after completing *The Covenant Signs, The Signs of Jonah,* and *The Signs of the Four Horsemen*, the new research regarding Mazzaroth signs provided additional Biblical astronomical evidence of our supernatural omnipotent Yahweh, God of Heaven. Therefore, this book has been revised, which turns the reader toward the Heavens just as God challenged Job and revealed His majesty and power to challenge him to repent and submit to God's will.

> [31]"Can you bind the chains of the Pleiades or loose the cords of Orion? [32]**Can you lead forth the Mazzaroth** in their season, or can you guide the Bear with its children? [33]Do you know the ordinances of the Heavens? Can you establish their rule on the Earth?   Job 38:31–33[2]

Each Sixth Seal Sign is covered in the order that was written by Apostle John on the Island of Patmos where he was given the Revelation of Jesus Christ.

What did John see? What was revealed to him?

Let's journey together through *The Sixth Seal Signs*.

Ender E. Law

3https://ephesians610.substack.com

For the perseverance of all the saints, be on the alert.

---

[2] The Holy Bible: English Standard Version (Job 38:31–33). (2016). Crossway Bibles.

Introduction

The Sixth Seal is a series of geological and astronomical signs that have fascinated theologians for centuries. This book will summarize literal correlations and calculate the probability of these signs occurring. The goal is to look at scripture as well as the unveiling of geological and astronomical events that parallel signs as described by the Apostle John in the Revelation of Jesus Christ.

This analysis is a literal Futurist/Premillennial view of Bible Prophecy which is the eschatological belief that Jesus will return in the near future. Other interpretations, including Postmillennial and A-Millennial do agree that Jesus will return in the end times and the hope is this book will speak to all saints that follow the commands of Jesus Christ as we look at actual geological and astronomical events.

First let's look at why God created the Heavens.

> 14 Then God said, "Let there be lights in the expanse of the Heavens to separate the day from the night, and let them be for signs and for seasons and for days and years; (Genesis 1:14, NASB1995)

God created the lights in Heaven for *signs and seasons*. These signs and seasons are time markers, warnings, and significant periods of time, much like a road sign tells us that an exit is up ahead, or that we should slow down or speed up to the recommended speed limit for our own safety.

Seasons in context to the original language did not mean spring, summer, fall, and winter but it meant this period was or is important and to pay attention and be watchful for God is showing His power and revealing His plans.[3]

The following is quoted from Ken Fleming's 2012 book, *God's Voice in the Stars: Zodiac Signs and Bible Truth.*

---

[3] Fleming, K. (2012). God's Voice in the Stars. Emmaus Worldwide. p. 11.

The word seasons (Hebrew *moed*) means something fixed or appointed. This word is never used in Scripture of a season of the year such as summer (a different word is alway used).[4]

"*Signs and seasons*" were therefore ordained by God to indicate happenings and the periods of time pertaining to them. God designed the stars with a purpose of using them prophetically to signify specific historical incidents at chosen times which would come to pass as the plan of salvation was unfolded.[5]

The Mazzaroth

Ken Fleming was a missionary in South Africa for the Zulu people from 1977 to 2002 and on the faculty emeritus for Emmaus Bible College, Dubuque, Iowa. His book *God's Voice in the Stars: Zodiac Signs and Bible Truth* describes the constellations, or Mazzaroth as quoted in the oldest book of the Bible, Job. In the book of Job, God answered Job out of the whirlwind with the following questions:

> [31] Canst thou bind the sweet influences of Pleiades, or loose the bands of Orion?
>
> [32] Canst thou bring forth **Mazzaroth** in his season? or canst thou guide Arcturus with his sons?
>
> Job 38:31-32, KJV
>
> [31] "Can you bind the chains of the Pleiades,
>
> Or loose the cords of Orion?
>
> [32] "Can you lead forth a [j] **constellation [Hebrew Mazzaroth]** in its season,
>
> And guide the Bear with her satellites [sons]?

---

[4] Ibid.

[5] Ibid.

Both the KJV and the NASB1995 versions are included to show that the Mazzaroth is Hebrew for constellations. The constellations were brought forth or led forth or named by God. God challenged Job, letting him know that only the God of Heaven and Earth can bring forth the Mazzaroth and specifically names the constellations, Orion and Pleiades. Arcturus is a star in the constellation Bootes. Some translators in NASB1995 equated it to the Bears, namely Ursa Major and Minor.

Job lived ~2200 BC which would put him on Earth during the time of Noah and his sons. If the stars and constellations were named during the time of Noah, then could they have been named prior to the flood? This is the compelling case presented by Mr. Fleming as he states:

> The grand truth is that God made the stars for a witness to mankind of a coming Redeemer who would save fallen man from the clutches of the enemy, destroy the enemy and his power, and finally establish a kingdom of righteousness and light. We shall show in the succeeding chapters that as states so beautifully in Psalm 89:37, God's witness in the sky is faithful.[6]

Could the constellations have been created and named by God as a means to tell the Gospel story?

> 37 "It shall be established forever like the moon,
>
> And the *witness in the sky* is faithful." *Selah.*
>
> Psalm 89:37, NASB1995

This is not to say we should worship the stars or live by them as an occult horoscope. No, God clearly doesn't want us to worship the sun, moon, or stars such as the pagan sun god, moon goddess, or planets Jupiter, Mars, Saturn, Venus... all worshipped by pagan nations.

However, could God in a pre-flood world, where there was no light pollution and smog, have placed the Heavenly bodies as a witness? Imagine fathers and mothers, with their sons and daughters, telling the

---

6 Fleming, K.C. (2025). God's Voice in the Stars: Zodiac Signs and Bible Truth. https://www.amazon.com/Gods-Voice-Stars-Zodiac-Signs/dp/1593871651

story of the Gospel through a huge "felt board" using the stars and constellations as they slept on rooftops or out in the fields tending their sheep.

God is Alpha and Omega, Beginning and the End. He is the First and the Last. Yes, then if we take His words literally, He named the stars and brought forth the constellations.

> He counts the number of the stars; He gives names to all of them. Psalm 147:4

Let's entertain the idea that God did create these constellations as signs and seasons, before there was the written Word of God.

Revelation 12 Sign: A Woman Giving Birth

> And **a great sign appeared in Heaven**: a woman clothed with the sun, with the moon under her feet, and on her head a crown of twelve stars. She was pregnant and was crying out in birth pains and the agony of giving birth.
>
> Revelation 12:1-2, ESV[7]

Here is a high-level description of Revelation 12:1-2 as some do believe it is a unique alignment that literally appeared in Heaven. On September 23rd, 2017, the following appeared: a woman clothed with the sun, the moon at her feet, 12 stars above her head, and she was giving birth. This was represented by Virgo the virgin and Leo the lion with Jupiter (spinning in retrograde) in the virgin's womb for 9 months. Jupiter happens to exit her womb on September 23rd, 2017[8]. The Revelation 12 sign on September 23rd, 2017 can be viewed using Stellarium astronomy software[9] or an equivalent. The screenshot (inverted) has been taken without the horizon to provide a full view of the alignment. The 12 stars, including 3 planets were visible in the constellation Leo at dawn on September 23rd,

---

[7] The Holy Bible: English Standard Version (Re 12:1–2). (2016). Crossway Bibles.

[8] Clarke, S. (2014-2016). https://www.youtube.com/watch?v=Rvkzpy7tOsQ

[9] https://stellarium.org/

2017. Then Virgo with Jupiter and the Moon were visible after the sun sets on the same day. The sun is "pinned" to her shoulder. Jupiter is hovering very close to Spica, in the bundle of wheat or barley, which is clutched in the left hand of the woman. Spica is interpreted as "seed" or "branch".

Furthermore, Robert Scott Wadsworth describes the star, Spica, as Tsemech (Hebrew), which is used exclusively in five Biblical references to describe the "Branch" (Isaiah 4:2, Jeremiah 23:5, 33:15, Zech 3:8, 6:12) which represents Messiah as the Branch.[10]

Fig. I1: The Revelation 12 Woman Sign

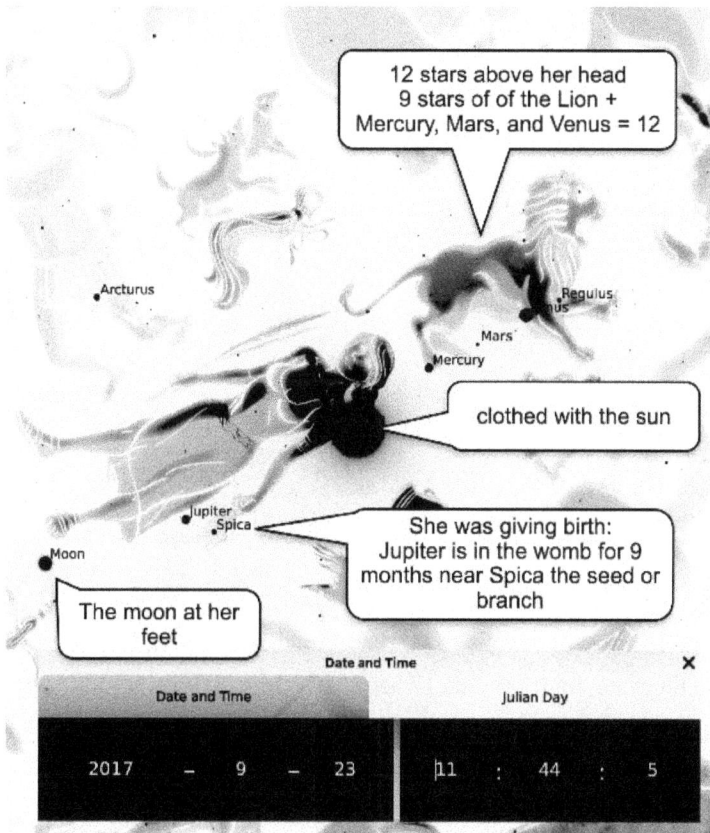

(source: Screenshot of Stellarium on 9/23/2017)

[10] Wadsworth, R. S. (2021). The Biblical Meanings of the Constellations and Planets. https://youtu.be/gVlfLAyDB34?si=K-ZFaYlLhZ06Ox4u&t=642

Revelation 12 Another Sign: A Dragon

Fig. I2: The Revelation 12 Draconids Sign

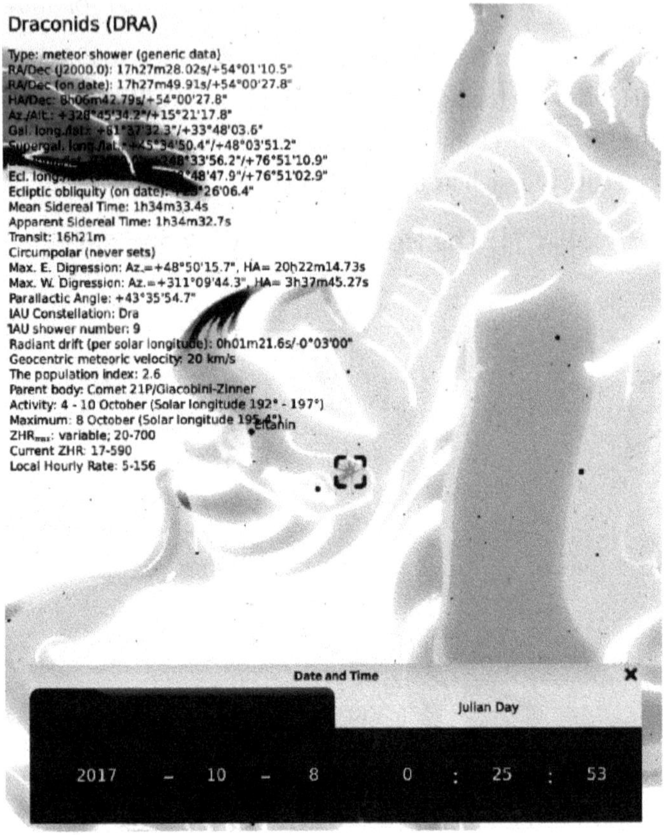

Draconids (DRA)

Type: meteor shower (generic data)
RA/Dec (J2000.0): 17h27m28.02s/+54°01'10.5"
RA/Dec (on date): 17h27m49.91s/+54°00'27.8"
HA/Dec: 8h06m42.79s/+54°00'27.8"
Az./Alt.: +328°45'34.2"/+15°21'17.8"
Gal. long./lat.: +61°37'32.3"/+33°48'03.6"
Supergal. long./lat.: +5°54'50.4"/+48°03'51.2"
[illegible]: +248°33'56.2"/+76°51'10.9"
Ecl. long. [illegible]: +48°47.9"/+76°51'02.9"
Ecliptic obliquity (on date): +23°26'06.4"
Mean Sidereal Time: 1h34m33.4s
Apparent Sidereal Time: 1h34m32.7s
Transit: 16h21m
Circumpolar (never sets)
Max. E. Digression: Az.=+48°50'15.7", HA= 20h22m14.73s
Max. W. Digression: Az.=+311°09'44.3", HA= 3h37m45.27s
Parallactic Angle: +43°35'54.7"
IAU Constellation: Dra
IAU shower number: 9
Radiant drift (per solar longitude): 0h01m21.6s/-0°03'00"
Geocentric meteoric velocity: 20 km/s
The population index: 2.6
Parent body: Comet 21P/Giacobini-Zinner
Activity: 4 - 10 October (Solar longitude 192° - 197°)
Maximum: 8 October (Solar longitude 195.4°)
ZHR$_{max}$: variable; 20-700
Current ZHR: 17-590
Local Hourly Rate: 5-156

Date and Time

Julian Day

2017 — 10 — 8   0 : 25 : 53

(source: Screenshot of Stellarium on 10/8/2017)

This next sign also seems to be played out in Heaven. There are two possible theories, both include Draco the Dragon. One includes Draco and the Draconids. Another theory includes Draco the Dragon, Scorpius and all serpent related constellations.

> And **another sign appeared in Heaven**: behold, a great red dragon, with seven heads and ten horns, and on his heads

seven diadems. His tail swept down a third of the stars of Heaven and cast them to the Earth. Revelation 12:3-4[11]

Hypothesis #1: The fiery red dragon, the serpent of old, Satan, may be represented by Draco the dragon. The Draconids peaked in 2017 and 2018 and will peak again in 2025 at over 500 meteors per hour. This correlation to Draco was made when analyzing the unique intensity of the Draconids which this book will cover in detail.

Fig. I3: The Revelation 12 Dragon, Serpents, & Scorpions

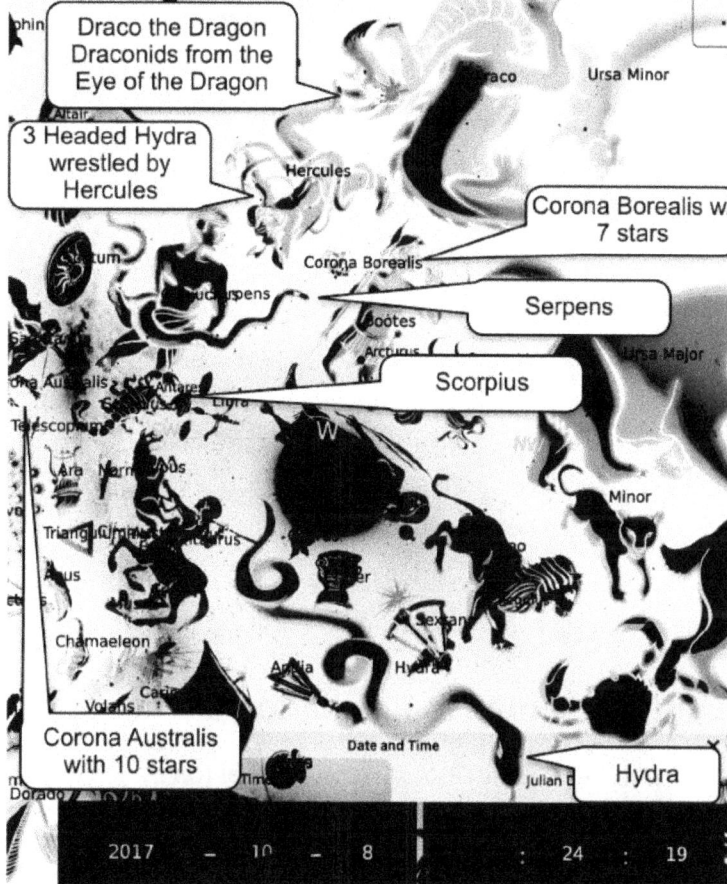

Hypothesis #2: The fiery red dragon, can also be correlated to all the constellations tied to a scorpion, serpent, and dragon which represent war,

---

[11] The Holy Bible: English Standard Version (Re 12:3–4). (2016). Crossway Bibles.

Serpent of Old and Satan, respectively. Counting the seven heads of the "dragon" include Draco, the 3-headed hydra wrestling Hercules, Serpens wrestling Ophiucus, Scorpius, and Hydra. Seven diadems parallels Corona Borealis with 7 primary stars, which is being pursued by Serpens and at the right shoulder of Bootes. Furthermore there are 10 horns including Draco (4 horns), Taurus, Aries, and Capricorn.

Global Events After the Revelation 12 Signs

These Heavenly signs were followed by other global events, geological and astronomical events:

- 2017 - Jerusalem was recognized as the capital of Israel

- 2018 - Israel celebrates 70 years as a nation - to be covered in detail in the next chapter on the Fig Tree generation.

- October, 2018 - The Draconids meteor storm peaked (more details will be covered in future chapters).

- For the next few years, from 2017 to 2020, Israel was protected and supported through various peace treaties and military operations. This included the Abraham Accords, recognizing the Golan Heights, and the sale of the F-22 Raptor. Furthermore, in 2025, additional peace treaties are being negotiated between Israel and Gaza.

When one studies Revelation, especially Chapters 12 and 13, events seem to align with signs in Heaven and on Earth.

The Four Horsemen in Revelation 6

The events in Revelation 12 and 13 also parallel Revelation 6 which begins with the Seals and the Four Horsemen. This research inspired over 80 articles on substack which led to the writing of a fourth book, *The Signs of the Four Horsemen - An Investigation of the Four Creatures, Horsemen, and the Armor of God through a Mazzaroth Lens,* which was published in 2025. In this book there is a detailed analysis of Sagittarius, the horseman with a bow and crown, as potentially what Apostle John was associating with the First Horseman that conquers. Scorpius the scorpion, is highlighted with the ancient Chinese fiery red star Antares, which is associated with the Second Horseman of war. Libra, a pair of scales, is carried by the Third Horseman. Finally, Capricorn, the half fish half goat constellation, is associated with the Fourth Horseman or Death followed by Hades. One finding is that Capricorn in Greek Mythology is the god Pan, who was hunted down by the monster Typhon from Tartaros deep below Hades[12].

Upon these constellations is found very compelling signs where sun, moon, and planets align to warn of spiritual warfare. In the book, *The Signs of the Four Horsemen*, these signs are on specific dates that align, to the day, with specific events on Earth pertaining to the tyrannical lockdowns and mandates experienced between 2020 and beyond.

Fig. 14: The Mazzaroth and the Four Horsemen

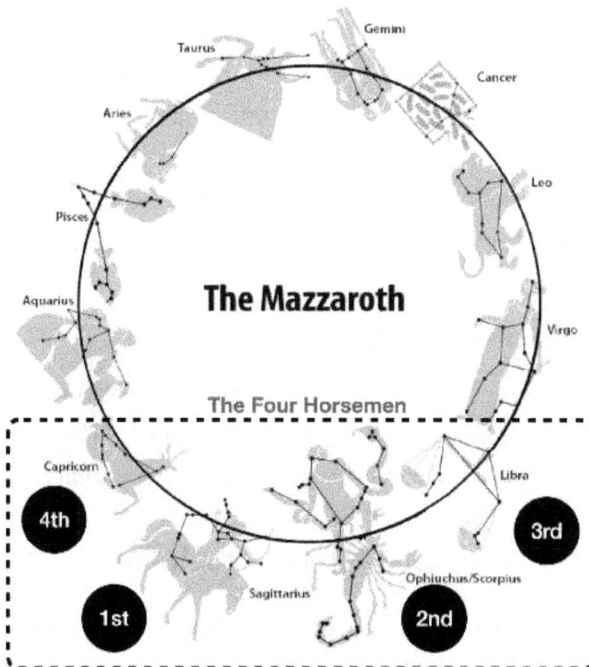

---

[12] https://www.theoi.com/Gigante/Typhoeus.html

Meanwhile in Revelation 6, after the Four Horsemen, which corresponds with the first four Seals, there is a fifth Seal where John is taken to Heaven to see the alter and souls slain. Finally, John describes the Sixth Seal which is the subject of this book.

The Sixth Seal in Revelation 6

The Sixth Seal of Revelation describes a series of geological and astronomical events described in scripture:

> [12] When he opened the sixth seal, I looked, and behold, there was a great Earthquake, and the sun became black as sackcloth, the full moon became like blood, [13] and the stars of the sky fell to the Earth as the fig tree sheds its winter fruit when shaken by a gale. [14] The sky vanished like a scroll that is being rolled up, and every mountain and island was removed from its place. [15] Then the kings of the Earth and the great ones and the generals and the rich and the powerful, and everyone, slave and free, hid themselves in the caves and among the rocks of the mountains, [16] calling to the mountains and rocks, "Fall on us and hide us from the face of him who is seated on the throne, and from the wrath of the Lamb, [17] for the great day of their wrath has come, and who can stand?"
>
> Revelation 6:12-17, ESV[13]

This book will focus in on the geological and astronomical signs described in the passage above in chronological order. First let's look at a couple terms, namely *temporal and geographical proximity*.

Mountain Peaks and Movie Trailers

Before we dive into analyzing *The Sixth Seal Signs* of bible prophecy let's review the following analogies which are inspired by *The Prophecy*

---

[13] The Holy Bible: English Standard Version (Re 6:12–17). (2016). Crossway Bibles.

Pros' Illustrated Guide to Tough Questions About the End Times, *By: Jeff Kinley, Todd Hampson.*[14]

You are the driver on a highway heading into the mountains and you are trying to tell your family how long before you get to the next campground. You are excited to see the mountains getting closer but the distance is difficult to judge and you still have a long way to go. There are two analogies:

Analogy 1: Mountain Peaks: The mountain highway pass illustrates "temporal and geographical proximity". As one drives down the highway toward the mountains, distance is misleading. One may think they are closer than they really are. There is sometimes no way to really know the temporal/geographical proximity between events until you have passed the event and look back at the time marker.

Temporal Proximity Example: For example we've passed what some say is a significant Revelation 12 sign in Heaven. September 23rd, 2017 there was a great sign in Heaven, the woman clothed with the sun, the moon at her feet, she was giving birth, and there were twelve stars above her head. If this sign is true, then it sets a time marker for where we could be according to a literal interpretation of Revelation. We now can look for other events in bible prophecy within relative "temporal proximity".

Geographical Proximity Example: For example the distance the event is from Israel. The recent Earthquake in Turkey and Syria is relatively close to Israel compared to other natural disasters.

Referencing Legal Definitions:

- *Temporal proximity:* is simply a legal term that is used to describe events that occurred relatively close to each other.[15]

---

[14] Kinley, J. & Hampson, T. (2021). The Prophet Pros' Illustrated Guide to Tough Questions About the End Times. Harvest House Publishers.

[15] https://www.hayberlawfirm.com/2020/03/10/what-is-temporal-proximity-and-how-can-it-be-used-to-help-prove-wrongful-termination/

- *Geographical Proximity*: In its simplest definition is the number of meters or kilometers that separate two entities.[16]

Analogy 2: Movie Trailer: Bible Prophecy is also like a Movie Trailer. The trailer shows rapid clips of the movie. In the same way Apostle John, is given a series of images to be written down in Revelation.

The order of these images given to John such as the Four Horsemen (Revelation 6), Beast of the Sea, and Beast of the Earth (Revelation 13), may **not** be in chronological order. The images may be occurring in parallel. The movie trailer is an invitation for you to see the full movie. The passages of bible prophecy are an invitation to dig deeper, to ponder in prayer, to look at world events, to study geographic proximity, to research historical context, to analyze original languages, to analyze Heavenly signs (like the Magi), and to prepare for what God has in store for us.

End Times or Eschatology Interpretations

Before going to see a movie, one may read reviews which will influence one's perception of the movie. In the same way, one may listen to someone else's interpretation of bible prophecy, end times, and/or eschatology. There are multiple views:

- Idealist - Revelation is an allegory.

- Historicist - Revelation aligns with church history.

- Preterist - Revelation happened already immediately after the life of Jesus Christ.

- Futurist - Revelation describes things that are happening or are to come.

- A-millennial - Revelation is symbolic, an allegory.

- Post-millennial - Revelation will not occur until all are reached through the Gospel.

---

[16] cairn.info/revue-journal-of-innovation-economics-2014-2-page-83

- Pre-millennial - Revelation describes a futurist great tribulation yet to come.

- Pre-tribulation rapture - A rapture occurs before the 7-year tribulation.

- Post-tribulation - A rapture occurs after the 7-year tribulation.

- Mid-tribulation or Pre-wrath - A rapture occurs in the middle of the 7 years or before the Wrath of God.

- No Rapture - A futurist interpretation where the saints will persevere through tribulation and be supernaturally protected.

How one interprets Revelation will influence one's perception of the world around them so it is important to study the Word personally. Establish a biblical world view based upon being alert and watchful for the return of Jesus Christ.

Each person comes into the discussion with the interpretations they have been taught by their parents and pastors which they have not questioned through years of sermons, books, and movies. Let's step back, and set aside institutional teachings held strongly by different denominations, priests, and pastors, and analyze the biblical text as well as the signs on a personal level.

This book will attempt to analyze and interpret the signs from a scriptural and literal perspective, calculate the probability of the individual sign and determine the overall statistical probability of these independent events.

Again you may ask the question why? Because for some, like Apostle Thomas, they need to see the holes in the hands and side of the risen Jesus. Some need to see the science and the math to build up their faith, to realize they need to put on the Full Armor of God (Ephesians 6:11) for the days are not getting any easier and the serpent of old, the dragon, Satan is trying to deceive those who follow the commands of Jesus Christ.

One Day is a 1000 years

When we study the Sixth seal, many have read this literally as events that all occur simultaneously on one day. In other words, some catastrophic event occurs that causes: an Earthquake, a solar eclipse, a blood moon, and a meteor shower in ONE day?

Imagine John is given a vision by Jesus to write down and he sees flashes of images before him which all seem merged together sequentially. Yet what if these are not necessarily events that occur on one day, but are events that occur over a period of years in relatively close temporal proximity. Also in God's timepiece, 3 years is just a few minutes. In 2 Peter 3, Peter states the following in context to the last days,

> *Know this first of all, that in the last days mockers will come with their mocking, following after their own lusts, and saying, "Where is the promise of His coming?* For ever since the fathers fell asleep, all continues just as it was from the beginning of creation." For when they maintain this, it escapes their notice that **by the word of God the Heavens existed long ago and the Earth was formed out of water and by water, through which the world at that time was destroyed, being flooded with water. But by His word the present Heavens and Earth are being reserved for fire, kept for the day of judgment and destruction of ungodly men.**
>
> 2 Peter 3:3-7, NASB1995

Note Peter writes that ungodly men will be judged and their destruction will not be a Great Flood as in the Days of Noah, but in the futurist interpretation the Wrath of God will be by fire. This is very interesting as scientifically in this book we will be looking at solar flares and events like the Carrington Event. The passage continues with some interesting numbers which many have tried to interpret:

> But **do not let this one fact escape your notice**, beloved, that **with the Lord one day is like a thousand years, and a thousand years like one day.** The Lord is not slow about His

promise, as some count slowness, but is patient toward you, **not wishing for any to perish but for all to come to repentance.** 2 Peter 3:8-9, NASB1995

God definitely wants to give all enough time to repent.

Applying some Algebra 1:

1 day = 1000 years

1 day = 24 hours = 1440 minutes

Hypothetically using 2 Peter 3:8

1000 years = 1440 minutes, as

1 year = 1440 minutes/1000 = 1.44 minutes

Thus, 2 years = ~3 minutes for God

> Side note: Similarly 20 years = ~30 minutes for God (Future Note: Could this be the 30 minutes referred to in Revelation 8?). Ok back to Revelation 6.

So what if from 2023 to 2025, ~3 minutes for God, the events all occur sequentially? Starting with an Earthquake in Turkey, followed by three more astronomical events. Do the following events align literally with Revelation 6:12-13, the opening of the Sixth Seal?

1. February 6th, 2023 - A Great Earthquake

2. April 8th, 2024 - A Total Solar Eclipse

3. March 13-14th, 2025 - A Blood Moon (future chapters will analyze 2 blood moons in 2025)

4. November 5th to December 16th, 2025 - ~12 Meteor Showers (future chapters will focus in on the October Draconids)

In this series, we will be analyzing each of the above events.

Listed below are events that lead up to The Sixth Seal Signs:

1. Solar and Lunar Eclipses of August, 2017

2. September 23rd, 2017 - Revelation 12 Sign - a Great Wonder in Heaven - A woman.

3.   October, 2017 - Revelation 12 Sign - Another sign in Heaven - A dragon.

4.   2018 - Israel's 70th anniversary as a nation

5.   October, 2019 - Medicane (a Mediterranean hurricane)

6.   December 20, 2020 - The Great Conjunction of Jupiter and Saturn - Israel becomes the world's laboratory

7.   March 1st-2nd, 2023 - The Great Conjunction of Jupiter and Venus - Revival spreads

All the signs above have occurred so we can analyze them in our rear view mirror as we drive down the highway of bible prophecy.

Revelation 6 the Sixth Seal - Terror?

The following requires great faith and prayer without fear. The Sixth Seal is labeled as "Terror" in NASB1995 so brace yourselves.

> The sky was split apart like a scroll when it is rolled up, and every mountain and island were moved out of their places. Then the kings of the Earth and the great men and the commanders and the rich and the strong and every slave and free man hid themselves in the caves and among the rocks of the mountains; and they said to the mountains and to the rocks, "Fall on us and hide us from the presence of Him who sits on the throne, and from the wrath of the Lamb; for the great day of their wrath has come, and who is able to stand?" Revelation 6:14-17, NASB1995

What does this picture mean? The "sky split apart like a scroll"?

Let's dive in, starting first with the Fig Tree Parable.

Chapter 1. The Fig Tree Parable: Is it a sign?

- What is the Fig Tree Parable?

- What is a generation?

- What do the Synoptic Gospels say?

1.1 The Fig Tree Generation in Scripture

This chapter will be allocated to the Fig Tree Parable as this is a sign potentially linked to the nation of Israel. Let's review the scripture:

> "Now **learn the parable from the fig tree**: when its branch has already become tender and puts forth its leaves, you know that summer is near; so, you too, when you see all these things, recognize that He is near, right at the door. Truly I say to you, **this generation will not pass away until all these things take place.** Heaven and Earth will pass away, but My words will not pass away. Matthew 24:32, NASB1995

What is a generation? This will be analyzed in the next chapter.

> "But of that **day and hour no one knows**, not even the angels of Heaven, nor the Son, but the Father alone. For the coming of the Son of Man will be just like the **days of Noah**. For as in those days before the flood they were eating and drinking, marrying and giving in marriage, until the day that Noah entered the ark, and they did not understand until the flood came and took them all away; so will the coming of the Son of Man be. Then there will be two men in the field; one will be taken and one will be left. 41 Two women will be grinding at the mill; one will be taken and one will be left. Matthew 24:36-41, NASB1995

If read out of context, the above verse can be misinterpreted as the rapture of the church. However, if read in context, this is referring to a coming day like the Days of Noah, in which people experienced God's Wrath, the Great Flood So John equates God's Wrath of the flood to when the Son of Man comes again. Some will suffer God's Wrath and some will not.

> "Therefore **be on the alert**, for you do not know which day your Lord is coming. Matthew 24:42, NASB1995

We must be on alert and watchful. We do not know the day or the hour of the second coming of Jesus Christ, but we surely must be ready for Jesus, the Son of Man, is coming again.

> But be sure of this, that if the head of the house had known at what time of the night the thief was coming, he would have been on the **alert** and would not have allowed his house to be broken into. **For this reason you also must be ready; for the Son of Man is coming at an hour when you do not think He will.** Matthew 24:43-44, NASB1995

This book will attempt to equip the saints to be **ready and alert**. For example, another significant event is the 70th anniversary of Israel. The fig tree is associated symbolically with Israel. Israel was recognized as a nation in 1948. A generation is 70 to 80 years.

> 1948 + 70 years = 2018
>
> 1948 + 75 years = 2023
>
> 1948 + 80 years = 2028

We now have another time marker in very close temporal proximity to the 2017 Revelation 12 sign in Heaven.

1.2 State of Israel is Born (May, 1948)

Jewish Awareness Ministries, an organization that focuses on proclaiming the Messiah to the Jews, preaching the Word, and praying for Israel, stated the following,

The Jewish people – who had been without a homeland for over 1,800 years would once again be a nation; they would once again have a home!

Attempt to place yourself in the sandals of one of those captives, of those who were expelled from Israel in the 2nd century A.D.

What if you, and your descendants, would subsequently remain in exile from your homeland for the following 1,800 years? This [the State of Israel] was a miracle of "Biblical proportions" for sure![17]

After 70 years from 1948 to 2018, S. Solomon writes in *The Times of Israel*, "The blooming of the desert: Key stages of Israel's economic growth"

The establishment of the state in 1948 and the absorption of immigrants: [806,000 to 8.84 million including 3.2 million immigrants over the years]

Financial institutions and fiscal restraint: Israeli leaders set up economic institutions including [banks, securities, etc.] to shield it from crises.

The tech industry in numbers: In the 20-year period of 1997-2017, 16,000 high-tech companies were set up, of which 8,000 are currently active.

The discovery of offshore natural gas reserves off Israel's coast has been a game-changer for the economy

Israel's economy had a gross domestic product (GDP) per capita of some $5,000 when the state was established in May 1948. The GDP per capita is today some $40,000[18]

---

[17] https://www.jewishawareness.org/70-years-israel-as-a-nation-1947-2017/

[18] https://www.timesofisrael.com/hold-for-wed-5-pm-the-growth-of-israels-economy-a-timeline/

Israel bloomed from a barren dry desert to now a flourishing and prosperous land. Amir Tsarfati, a globally known speaker on Israel and Bible Prophecy conferences, The Fig Tree is Blooming (a 1 minute video), states, "We are the generation, that will not pass away, because we see the fig tree blooming!" (Amir Tsarfati, Youtube)[19]

1.3 The Fig Tree Parable

Let's look at the following parable from the Synoptic Gospels (i.e.: Mark, Matthew, and Luke) when the disciples asked Christ about the things to come and the future return of Jesus Christ, Jesus responds with the fig tree parable. The Synoptic Gospels are nearly identical with slight differences. Note Luke writes "fig tree and all the trees" vs. "fig tree".

> [28] "Now learn the parable from the **fig tree**: when its branch has already become tender and puts forth its leaves, you know that summer is near. [29] Even so, you too, when you see these things happening, recognize that He is near, *right* at the door. Mark 13:28-29, NASB1995

> [29] Then He told them a parable: "Behold the **fig tree and all the trees**; [30] as soon as they put forth *leaves*, you see it and know for yourselves that summer is now near. [31] So you also, when you see these things happening, recognize that the kingdom of God is near. Luke 21:29-31, NASB1995

> [32] "Now learn the parable from the **fig tree**: when its branch has already become tender and puts forth its leaves, you know that summer is near; [33] so, you too, when you see all these things, recognize that He is near, *right* at the door. Matthew 24:32-33, NASB1995

Some bible scholars interpret fig trees symbolically as a representation of Israel (Hosea 9:10; Joel 1:6–7).

---

[19] Tsarfati, A. (2023). [Youtube] Amir Tsarfati: The Fig Tree is Blooming. Behold Israel with Amir Tsarfati. https://www.youtube.com/watch?v=plFAl978vJl

Craig John Lovik is an American writer and theologian. He made a significant contribution to family literature and wrote several important books on religion. Mr. Lovik narrates the following animation explaining The Fig Tree Prophecy. The screenshot below illustrates the fig tree as Israel which becomes a nation on May 14th, 1948 and a generation which will see the Second Coming of Jesus Christ.

Notice also Luke's addition "behold the fig tree and all the trees" (Luke 21:29). Why did Luke include "and all trees"?[20] What else could all the trees mean? C.J. Lovik's video explains that when the Ottoman Empire was dismantled, many nation state borders were redrawn and each nation had their own specific tree including: Lebanon (1943) Cedar Tree, Syria (1943) Olive Tree, Jordan (1946) Palm Tree, Saudi Arabia (1932) Date Palm Tree, and Israel (1948) Fig Tree.

Each tree blossomed as the nations were established bordering Israel. Could this have been the reference to "and all trees?".(C.J. Lovik, 2021)[21]

Let's look next at what Amir Tsarfati meant when he said, "This generation, will not pass"?

1.4 What Generation?

> [30] Truly I say to you, **this generation will not pass away** until all these things take place. Mark 13:30 NASB1995[22]

> [34] Truly I say to you, **this generation will not pass away** until all these things take place. Matthew 24:34 NASB1995[23]

> [32] Truly I say to you, **this generation will not pass away** until all things take place. Luke 21:32 NASB1995[24]

---

[20] https://www.bibleref.com/Mark/13/Mark-13-28.html

[21] Ibid.

[22] https://my.bible.com/bible/100/MRK.13.30

[23] https://my.bible.com/bible/100/MAT.24.34

[24] https://my.bible.com/bible/100/LUK.21.32

Who is the generation that will not pass away until they see the 2nd coming of Jesus Christ?

> *Genea* (Ancient Greek)
>
> In Ancient Greek, generation is *genea* from biblehub.com
>
> genea: race, family, generation
>
> Original Word: γενεά, ᾶς, ἡ[25]

or from wiktionary:

> **γενεά** · (geneá) f (genitive **γενεᾶς**); first declension 1. birth, 2. race, descent, 3. generation, 4. offspring[26]

Words derived from *genea* include gene and genetics. This generation has many definitions which will not be listed here but can be referenced on wiktionary.

There is no specific time boundary for the word *generation* other than ~30 years, the time it takes for a person to be born and have children. However, in the Synoptic Gospels it states **"this generation will not pass away until all these things take place".** This would imply the lifespan of this generation and not just 30 to 40 years. What is an average lifespan?

> What is the typical Lifespan?
>
> 10 As for the days of our life, they contain **seventy years, Or if due to strength, eighty years**, Yet their pride is but labor and sorrow; For soon it is gone and we fly away. Psalms 90:10 NASB1995

In Psalms, it states that a typical lifespan of an individual is 70 to 80 years. Before Noah and the Great Flood, lifespans were much longer, but since the flood the average lifespan has been ~75. Harvard Health states the following:

---

[25] https://biblehub.com/greek/1074.htm

[26] https://en.wiktionary.org/wiki/%CE%B3%CE%B5%CE%BD%CE%B5%CE%AC#Ancient_Greek

With rare exceptions, life expectancy has been on the rise in the US: it was 47 years in 1900, 68 years in 1950, and by 2019 it had risen to nearly 79 years. But it fell to 77 in 2020 and dropped further, to **just over 76**, in 2021.[27]

Interestingly,

At an expected 84.4, Israelis will be ranked seventh in the world in longevity, moving up from their current 13th place spot (82.1).[28]

While globally the average is just over 70 at 72+ as of 2019.[29]

In ~2018, Pastor John MacArthur interpreted this parable from multiple views of eschatology.

When you **see the signs**, leaves, you know summer's near. And with summer comes fruit and harvest.

...great tribulation. The signs in the sun, the moon, the stars, on the Earth, the roaring of the sea and the waves, the powers of the Heavens shaken, people in dismay, perplexity, dying from fear...

But once those signs start, once they start, you can be sure that when you see these things happen, the Kingdom of God is near.

How near? "At the door," Mark 13:29. (MacArthur, J, 2017)[30]

Pastor MacArthur, then debates various views of the "the generation". He disagrees with the view that Jesus was referring to the immediate

---

[27] https://www.health.harvard.edu/blog/why-life-expectancy-in-the-us-is-falling-202210202835#:~:text=With%20rare%20exceptions%2C%20life%20expectancy,just%20over%2076%2C%20in%202021.

[28] https://www.timesofisrael.com/israel-ranks-7th-in-global-life-expectancy-rankings-for-2040/

[29] https://ourworldindata.org/life-expectancy/

[30] MacArthur, J. (2017). The Final Generation of the Future Judgment (Luke 21:29-33). Grace to You. https://www.youtube.com/watch?v=hbdRgl-JH0o

generation, who died ~70 A.D. and the Hal Lindsey view of a 40 year generation after 1948 who died in 1988 (i.e.: 1948+40 = 1988). He concludes that the generation who sees the *signs* will see the coming of Christ when He returns. In this sermon, Pastor MacArthur does not use the 70 to 80 year lifespan as noted by C.J. Lovik which comes from Psalms 90:10. Pastor MacArthur just simplifies the prophecy to those who see the *signs* will see the Second Coming in their lifespan. Note the full C.J. Lovik animated video, it is included as a footnote.[31]

Reference <u>Matthew 24:32-42, NASB1995</u>. If the fig tree is Israel and the other trees are the neighboring nations. Israel was recognized as a nation in 1948. A lifespan of this generation is 70 to 80 years.

- 1948 + 70 years = 2018
    - a year after the Revelation 12 signs in the Heaven
- 1948 + 75 years = 2023
    - 2023 is the year of the Earthquake in Turkey and Syria to be covered in the next chapter.
- 1948 + 80 years = 2028

We now have some high watch years to look for signs…

1.5 The Dewey Decimal System Analogy

Remember libraries with card catalogs that used the Dewey Decimal System? The system would help one search for books using the appropriate shelf, subject, and book. Now in our high-tech world we have search engines and in IT we have database queries and elastic search query languages, all to help us isolate and filter out noise to get to the data we need quickly and efficiently.

Is God giving us these parables and signs to help us search efficiently and quickly so we know when to look up?

---

[31] Lovik, C.J. (2021). The Fig Tree Prophecy (Animated). RockIslandBooks. https://www.youtube.com/watch?v=uTcoID_P89g&t=192s

The Year 1948, when Israel becomes a Nation is a significant sign on Earth. Israel, symbolized by the fig tree, is blooming and flourishing today. At this moment in history, we have a lifespan of 70 to 80 years as noted in **Psalms 90:10**. As of 2025, Israel has seen great war with Gaza and neighboring countries. Then on October 13th, 2025, "HISTORIC MOMENT. President Trump signs the Gaza Peace Plan for peace in the Middle East".[32]

There are other signs unfolding with temporal and geographical proximity (to be covered in the following chapters)

1.6 Scripture Review "Be Alert and Watchful"

Jesus states that we do not know the day or the hour, but we surely must stay alert. Read **Mark 13:28-47, NASB1995**.

> 28 "Now learn the **parable from the fig tree**: when its branch has already become tender and puts forth its leaves, you know that summer is near.
>
> 29 Even so, you too, when you see these things happening, recognize that He is near, right at the door.
>
> 30 **Truly I say to you, this generation will not pass away until all these things take place.**
>
> 31 Heaven and Earth will pass away, but My words will not pass away.
>
> 32 **But of that day or hour no one knows,** not even the angels in Heaven, nor the Son, but the Father alone.
>
> 33 "Take heed, **keep on the alert; for you do not know when the appointed time will come.** 34 It is like a man away on a journey, who upon leaving his house and putting his slaves in charge, assigning to each one his task, also commanded the doorkeeper **to stay on the alert.**

---

[32] https://www.whitehouse.gov/videos/historic-moment-president-trump-signs-the-gaza-peace-plan-for-peace-in-the-middle-east/

35 Therefore, **be on the alert**—for you do not know when the master of the house is coming, whether in the evening, at midnight, or when the rooster crows, or in the morning—

36 in case he should come suddenly and find you asleep.

37 What I say to you I say to all, '**Be on the alert!**'"

(Mark 13:33-37, NASB1995)

Jesus is stating that we will not know the day or the hour of His return. However, he states 4 times in this passage to be on the alert and watchful. There are actually two Greek words uses in Mark for "be on alert and be watchful".

In Mark 13:33, "keep on the alert" in Greek is *agrupneó* denoting to be sleepless, wakeful meaning I am not asleep but awake.[33] *Agrupneó* is used 4 times in the Bible, including,

36 But **keep on the alert at all times**, praying that you may have strength to escape all these things that are about to take place, and to stand before the Son of Man."

Luke 21:36, NASB1995

In Mark 13:34, "to stay on the alert" in Greek is *grégoreó* denoting to be awake, to watch.[34] *Grégoreó* is used 23 times in the Bible, including to the church of Sardis in the Revelation of Jesus Christ

Wake up, and strengthen the things that remain, which were about to die; for I have not found your deeds completed in the sight of My God. **So remember what you have received and heard; and keep it, and repent**. Therefore if you do not wake up, I will come like a thief, and you will not know at what hour I will come to you. Revelation 3:2-3, NASB1995

Therefore let's explore the signs to help us be watchful, alert, and vigilant.

---

[33] https://biblehub.com/greek/69.htm

[34] https://biblehub.com/greek/1127.htm

Chapter 2. Earthquakes and Comets

2025 Update: This chapter has been supplemented with research which investigated a correlation between seismic activity such as Earthquakes and volcanoes with passing comets.

- What Earthquake occurred in 2023?

- What does this have to do with comets?

- What comet came close to the Earth in 2023?

2.1 2023 Major Earthquakes in Turkey and Syria

On February 6th, 2023, hundreds of years of pressure was released in southern Turkey and northern Syria traveling along the fault lines.

> *We pray for all that have been impacted through death, injuries, and displacement.*

As of July 23rd, 2023, The confirmed death toll stands at 59,259: 50,783 in Turkey and 8,476 in Syria. The Earthquake is the deadliest in present-day Turkey since the 526 AD Antioch Earthquake, and the deadliest natural disaster in Turkey's modern history.[35]. In this article we will analyze and connect-the-dots on this natural disaster. Was this a sign?

The Wall Street Journal documentary describes the southern Turkey 7.8 magnitude quake hitting at 4:17AM followed by a second 7.5 magnitude Earthquake the next afternoon with more than 285 aftershocks which traveled down the coast of Syria and southern Turkey.[36]

You can take the Earth and divide it up into several large plates that are all moving around each other, and most Earthquakes occur at the

---

[35] https://en.wikipedia.org/wiki/2023_Turkey%E2%80%93Syria_Earthquake

[36] Wall Street Journal (2023). The Science Behind the Massive Turkey-Syria Earthquakes | WSJ. Wall Street Journal. youtube.com/watch?v=Hd4xCmuwiBw

boundaries between the plates. This one is called the Anatolia tectonic plate. It's actually a micro-plate due to its tiny size and it is constantly under pressure, being pressed upward against the Eurasia plate by the Arabia plate.

That pressure squeezes the Anatolia plate westward where it faces even more friction from the Africa plate, which is also moving upward.[37] The Anatolian micro-plate is caught in a vise between the Arabian plate moving to the north against the Eurasian plate, and this small plate is being pushed aside as a result of that motion. That means the boundaries between the Anatolia plate and the Africa and Arabia plates are trying to slide against each other as the Anatolia moves to the west and the Africa and Arabia move to the east.

These borders are called strike-slip faults. The friction builds up between the plates as they're pushed in different directions - until it's too much and they slip causing a strike-slip Earthquake.

The strain will build up and finally, **it will rupture and release all that accumulated strain in a large Earthquake**. That's what happened in Gazientep, resulting in that 7.8 magnitude quake. USGS estimates that the strike-slip occurred along about 100 miles of the fault.

These were significant Earthquakes for this fault system and experts assess it was caused by an accumulation of 300 to 500 years' worth of strain that's built up since the last Earthquake.

Experts say the energy released in that slip is comparable to that released during the explosive **1980 Mount St. Helen's volcanic eruption**.[38]

The Turkey and Syria Earthquake's death toll has been tragically climbing weekly as more victims are found under the rubble. When sorting

---

[37] Wall Street Journal (2023). The Science Behind the Massive Turkey-Syria Earthquakes | WSJ. Wall Street Journal. youtube.com/watch?v=Hd4xCmuwiBw

[38] Ibid.

all Earthquakes in the 21st century by death toll, it ranks as the 4th worst in history throughout the world.[39]

2.2 Geographical Proximity of the Earthquake

The distance from the Turkey/Syria Earthquake to Jerusalem is a 9+ hour drive south on the M5 freeway. Though the Earthquake epicenter was in Turkey it was still felt across the Middle East including Israel.[40]

The strike-slip fault accumulated hundred's of years of energy to rip a canyon right through an olive orchard. The picture below shows how the Earth slipped and ripped the olive tree rows in Antakya, Turkey.

Fig. 2.2: Turkey Olive Orchid Ripped Apart by Earthquake

(source: ITV News, Youtube)

Villagers thought it was an air raid: the sound of explosions created by cracking rock, the flashes by the sparks that flew as the Earth's crust was torn apart.... A young boy is interviewed, "It used to be a flat field I would ride my motorbike on it" said this boy, it was all an olive grove which is

---

[39] https://en.wikipedia.org/wiki/List_of_natural_disasters_by_death_toll

[40] https://www.haaretz.com/news/middle-east/2023-02-06/ty-article/Earthquake-of-magnitude-7-7-strikes-turkey-gfz/00000186-2458-d442-a18f-afd9a6cf0000

now bisected by a gorge that in places is the width of a football field, the rift is so deep that a 13-story building could fit in it[41]

As a side note we just covered the Fig Tree Parable in the previous article. C.J. Lovik's video explains that when the Ottoman Empire was dismantled, many nation state borders were redrawn and each nation had their own specific tree including Syria which has been represented as the olive tree. Along the Turkish and Syrian border there are many olive orchards and the region is well known for its olives and olive oil. Syria borders Turkey, Lebanon and Israel in geographical proximity.

2.3 Temporal Proximity of the Earthquake to a Comet

As an analogy, a libraries Dewey Decimal catalogue helps direct one to a particular book. Say one is looking for a Bible Prophecy book. One follows the sign: "230 Christianity" section which is a row of several shelves of books. Then search under 236.x for books on Eschatology (the study of end-times) and one can search for a specific book. Are the signs helping us find the "row, shelves, and the specific book" of the end-times?

God gives us parables and signs to help us be prepared so we know when to look up. Let's review the Fig Tree Parable. In 1948, Israel becomes a nation where it is symbolized by the fig tree blooming and flourishing. The generation that sees this will not pass. A lifespan of 70 to 80 years gives us a window of time to look for signs. We do not know the day or the hour but we surely will know the signs. At the 75 year mark from 1948 is 2023, the year of a great Earthquake. Is this coincidence?

Do the following events align literally with Revelation 6:12-13, the opening of the Sixth Seal?

1. February 6th, 2023 - A Great Earthquake and a Comet?

2. April 8th, 2024 - A Total Solar Eclipse

---

[41] ITV (2023). Turkey-Syria Earthquake ripped huge chasm in what was once an olive field near Antakya | ITV News. ITV. youtube.com/watch?v=liDvo-xTinY

3. 2025 A pair of Blood Moons to be researched, and

4. Meteor Showers (or the Draconids unique meteor shower pattern to be reviewed in this book).

One of these signs may be a wandering star, a comet?

2.4 Wandering Stars

The following is from excerpts of a substack article "The Book of Jude: Waves of the Sea, Wandering Stars, and the Seed of the Woman", published on October 11th, 2024.[42]

Jude, the brother of James and half-brother of Jesus Christ is believed to have written the Book of Jude. It is only a single chapter right before the Book of Revelation. Though Jude is very brief, it is filled with imagery. Jude makes apocalyptic references to the return of Jesus Christ and the punishment of the ungodly. A section in Jude is labeled "Judgement of False Teachers", but there is more here than just false teaching.

Jude writes,

> wild waves of the sea, casting up the foam of their own shame; **wandering stars**, for whom the gloom of utter darkness has been reserved forever.
>
> Jude 13, ESV

What are the "wandering stars"? *Wandering* (Greek: *planētēs*) is only used once in the entire Bible. Some believe *planētēs* is the origin of planets. However, ancients would track the planets and they soon learned they followed a predictable path through the tent of stars. This path is called the ecliptic as it traverses the 12 major constellations of the Mazzaroth. The Mazzaroth of stars travels in a large circular rotation around Polaris, the pole star. Sailors at sea and caravans in the desert could travel by the constellations moving like a giant wheel. The ancients could rely upon the sun, moon, and planets to mark their calendars, however, they could not rely upon the "wandering stars".

---

[42] https://ephesians610.substack.com/p/the-book-of-jude-waves-of-the-sea

Are Comets in the Bible? Comets have been researched at length from a "broom of destruction" (Isaiah 14:23) to volcanoes, Earthquakes, and war. *The International Standard Bible Encyclopaedia*, states the following on *wandering stars*,

> in Jude ver 13: "Wandering stars, for whom the blackness of darkness hath been reserved forever." These *astéres planétai [Greek]* **are not our "planets**," but either meteors or **comets, more probably the latter**, as meteors are more appropriately described as "falling stars."[6] [emphasis added]

Falling stars or meteor showers have been analyzed, similar to the Draconids. Meteors do not wander. They appear and streak across the sky in a blink of an eye. Comets leave dust particles that form the meteor showers.

2.5 Broom of Destruction

Isaiah documents the Lord declaring,

> "I will rise up against them," declares the Lord of hosts, "and will cut off from Babylon name and survivors, offspring and posterity," declares the Lord.
>
> "I will also make it a possession for the hedgehog and swamps of water, and
>
> I will sweep it with the **broom of destruction**," declares the Lord of hosts.
>
> Isaiah 14:22-23, NASB 1995 [emphasis added]

What is the "broom of destruction"? Is this just figurative, illustrating how God will sweep away evil?

"Broom" in Hebrew is *matate* (Strong's Concordance: 4292) which denotes broom or besom and it is only used once in the entire Bible.[43] *Besom* is a broom made of twigs and tied with twine around a stick.

---

[43] https://biblehub.com/hebrew/4292.htm

Coincidentally the *Dictionary of the Scots Language* translates "the fyrie-boosome" as a comet,

[O.Sc. has *bisom*, *bissom*, *bisem*, *bis(s)ome*, *byssome*, meaning a *besom* (lit.), and trs. also to a comet or its tail; *bussome* is also found in Dunbar: "the weido on ane bussome rydand" (*Lucina schynnyng in Silence of the Nicht*). Its variant *boosome*, used by Knox to describe a comet "the fyrie-boosome," has survived in the Gall. dialect.[44]

"Sweep" in Hebrew is *tu* or *tete* (Strong's Concordance: 2894) which denotes sweep and also it is only used once in the entire Bible.[45]

"Destruction" in Hebrew is *shamad* (Strong's Concordance: 8045) which denotes to be exterminated or destroyed and used 90 times in the Bible.[46]

Can Isaiah's "Broom of Destruction" be a "Comet of Destruction"?

In 1992, the late Hollis R. Johnson, astronomer and Professor at Indiana University, along with the late Svend Holm-Nielsen, theologian, published this theory in a paper titled, "Comments on two possible references to comets in the Old Testament."

Abstract: In a search for possible references to comets in the Old Testament, we found two candidates, one from the time of David and one from the time of Isaiah. Although no firm conclusions can be drawn, we discuss the linguistic, historical, and astronomical evidence for each.[47]

Though no firm conclusions can be drawn here, the linguistic, historical, and astronomical data points support the theological worldview.

---

[44] https://dsl.ac.uk/entry/snd00062604

[45] https://biblehub.com/hebrew/2894.htm

[46] https://biblehub.com/hebrew/8045.htm

[47] Johnson, H. R., & Holm-Nielsen, S. (1993). Comments on two possible references to comets in the old testament. *Scandinavian Journal of the Old Testament*, 7(1), 99–107. https://doi.org/10.1080/09018329308585009

Finally, another datapoint, Chinese astronomers, dating as far back as 1059 BC, called comets with a tail, *huixing* (彗星, "broom star"). The broomstick metaphor was evident in China as they observed the tails pointing away from the sun.[48]

2.6 Comets ~ Solar Activity ~ Seismic Activity

The following is an excerpt from the substack research article "1883 Krakatoa Volcanic Eruption, Solar Cycle 12, and the 12P Comet", posted May 3rd, 2024.[49]

Fig. 2.6: Prof Rickard News Clipping on Comet Affects

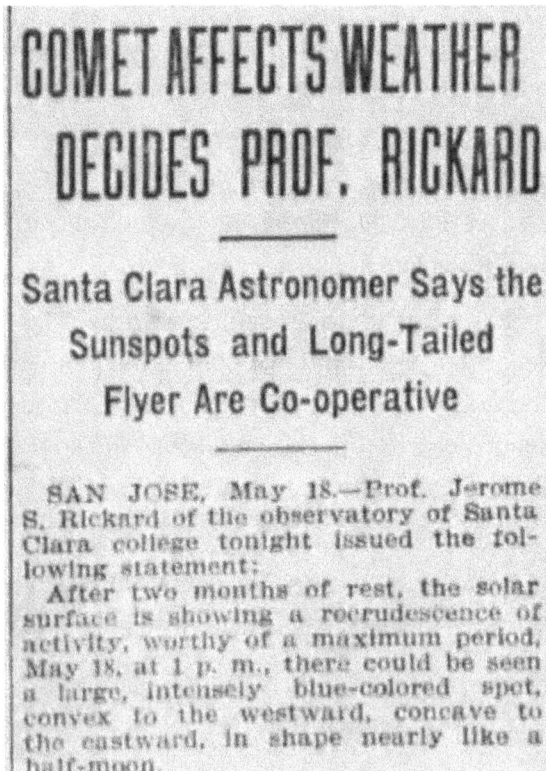

COMET AFFECTS WEATHER DECIDES PROF. RICKARD

Santa Clara Astronomer Says the Sunspots and Long-Tailed Flyer Are Co-operative

SAN JOSE, May 18.—Prof. Jerome S. Rickard of the observatory of Santa Clara college tonight issued the following statement:

After two months of rest, the solar surface is showing a recrudescence of activity, worthy of a maximum period, May 18, at 1 p. m., there could be seen a large, intensely blue-colored spot, convex to the westward, concave to the eastward, in shape nearly like a half-moon.

---

[48] https://en.wikipedia.org/wiki/
Historical_comet_observations_in_China#:~:text=Later%20on%2C%20a%20distin
ction%20is,point%20away%20from%20the%20sun.

[49] https://ephesians610.substack.com/p/1883-krakatoa-volcanic-eruption-solar

In 1910, published in the Los Angeles Herald, <u>Professor Jerome S. Rickard of the Observatory of Santa Clara College</u> shared that there is a cooperative relationship between comets and sunspots.

Father Jerome Sixtus Ricard was a Jesuit astronomer and meteorologist. Ricard was an outsider to the professional scientific community during his entire career, but he had enthusiasm, faith, and promotional ability.

Rickard of the observatory of Santa Clara College tonight issued the following statement, which correlated comets to solar and therefore Earth's seismic activity.

> After two months of rest, the solar surface is showing a recrudescence [the recurrence of an undesirable condition.] of activity, worthy of a maximum period...

> ...it is well nigh demonstrated, that the rise and the wane of sunspots and faculae [a bright region on the surface of the sun, linked to the subsequent appearance of sunspots in the same area.] is due to planetary influence. The greatest of the world's long-range forecasters is going by the planets' positions. I go by the sunspots and faculae. Our dates always agree.

> Therefore, planets and sunspots are indissolubly [in a way that is impossible to take apart or bring to an end, or that exists for a very long time] connected.

> Halley's Comet may be viewed and ranked as a formative planet. Therefore, it must have a reactive influence on the sun and consequently on the weather.[50]

Using some deductive reasoning, increasing sunspot activity increases the possibility of coronal mass ejections (CMEs). CMEs that are Earth-facing increase the chances of seeing Aurora Borealis and the possibility of seismic activity (to be analyzed in detail later in this book). Some comets

---

[50] https://www.newspapers.com/article/los-angeles-herald-comets-tail-split/21987990/

may impact sunspot activity, most likely through perturbation. Therefore, comets may be related to seismic activity through sunspots. Seismic activity, such as significantly large Earthquakes experienced in Turkey and Syria. Was there a comet in temporal proximity to the Earthquakes? Yes, the Green Comet of 2023.

2.7 "The Green Comet" aka C/2022 E3 (ZTF)

Comet C/2022 E3 (ZTF) is named using the International Astronomical Union standards, where "C/" refers to a non-periodic comet, which means it does not have an orbital period of less than 200 years, nor is it a comet that has been observed previously. "2022" is the year the comet was discovered. "E" indicates the half-month it was discovered. (The first half of January is A, the second half is B, so the first half of March is E.) "3" means it was the third comet discovered in that half-month. "ZTF" tells us it was discovered by the Zwicky Transient Facility at Palomar Observatory in California.[51]

The Green Comet of 2023 races in from the great expanse like a true wandering star and a "Broom of Destruction". Astronomers have not seen this intergalactic wanderer before, and some believe it may not return, or if it does, it will be tens of thousands to millions of years. The wandering star was discovered on March 2nd, 2022. It reached its closest point to the Sun on January 12th, 2023. The Green Comet will be at its closest point to Earth, and will be brightest in our skies, on February 1st, 2023, within one week of the Great Earthquake in Turkey and Syria on February 6th, 2023.

Father Jerome Ricard's hypothesis that comets may impact sunspots and solar activity may be correct. The Green Comet influenced our sun. Additional research will show that solar activity may be related to seismic activity, thus triggering the Turkey and Syria Earthquakes in 2023.

---

[51] https://www.timeanddate.com/news/astronomy/green-comet-2023

Chapter 3. Prophecy, Probability & Path through the Mazzaroth

2025 Update: This chapter has been supplemented with new research on the 2023 Green Comet's path through the Mazzaroth.

- Why is probability useful here?

- What is the path of the Green Comet?

- What Mazzaroth signs does it cross?

In Revelation Chapter 6, the 6th Seal, what are the odds of a Great Earthquake and similar aftershock?

> **Answer:** 1 in 60,000
>
> (Disclaimer: Assuming the 2nd M 7.5 Earthquake was an aftershock to the M 7.8)
>
> Show work below

3.1 Why Probability?

Yes, probability can be applied to the signs in Revelation. Each of the geological and astronomical signs in The Sixth Seal can be analyzed not just using the science behind them but also the question arises, are these events just coincidence? Earthquakes happen all the time, what is special about this particular Earthquake?

This book will attempt to take up the probability and prophecy challenge. The hope is the reader will find the results fascinating and faith building… maybe there is a chance that someone reading this series will be strengthened in their faith and belief in our Lord Jesus Christ and the reality of events unfolding.

This chapter will look at the scientific and mathematical probability of events that are being unveiled before us. Probability has been used by bible scholars to look at bible prophecy and apologetics for years. Here are a few references:

- January 7th, 2020 in Crosswalk.com: Dr. Roger Barrier "What Is the Probability of the Reality of Jesus Christ?"

- Christian Prophecy.org Lion and the Lamb Ministries: Dr. David Reagan "Applying the Science of Probability to the Scriptures"

- End Times Prophecy: Bible Prophecy and Probability

Dr. Harold Hartzler, an officer of the American Scientific Affiliation. writes,

> "What chance did Moses have when writing the first chapter [of Genesis] of getting thirteen items all accurate and in satisfactory order?" His calculations conclude it would be one chance in 31,135,104,000,000,000,000,000 (1 in 31 x 10^21).[52]

Let's consider using probability calculations with the signs that are being unveiled through our previous series: Revelation Chapter 6, the Sixth Seal.

> I looked when He broke the sixth seal, and
> there was a **great Earthquake**; and
> the **sun became black as sackcloth made of hair**, and
> **the whole moon became like blood**; and
> the stars of the sky fell to the Earth,
> as a fig tree casts its unripe figs when shaken by a great
> wind. The **sky was split apart like a scroll when it is rolled
> up**, and. **every mountain and island were moved out of their
> places.** Revelation 6:12-14, NASB1995

What is the probability that Apostle John documents signs which are sequenced in the following timeline?

---

[52] Reagan, D. (2023). "Applying the Science of Probability to the Scriptures". *Christian Prophecy.org Lion and the Lamb Ministries.* https://christinprophecy.org/articles/applying-the-science-of-probability-to-the-scriptures/

1. **2023 Great Earthquake(s)**

2. **2017 and 2024 Solar Eclipses**

3. **2025 Blood Moons**

4. **2018 and 2025 Meteor Showers/Storms**

5. **2023 to 2025+ Northern Lights/Coronal mass ejections**

6. **2023 to 2025+ More Earthquakes**

Let's start with the probability of #1, there was a great Earthquake".

3.2 Earthquake Probabilities

Earthquake Probabilities describe the long-term chances that an Earthquake of a certain magnitude will happen during a time window… These probabilities might range from 1-in-30 to 1-in-300.

For some faults, historical occurrences are not available, but rate of slip along the fault can be estimated. Assuming a particular magnitude, one can estimate the number of years it would take to accumulate the required amount of slip. This estimate can be used to give an annual rate and used in the same manner as historical rates. **These probabilities might range from 1-in-300 to 1–in-3000.**[53]

In 2023 there were two Earthquakes in Turkey and on the border of Syria:

1. February 5th, 2023 - Magnitude 7.8 Pazarcik

2. February 6th, 2023 - Magnitude 7.5 Elbistan

USGS states,

> About **one in every 20 large-magnitude Earthquakes** will have a similar-sized aftershock near it within the first week. That was the case in Turkey, with the M7.8 mainshock being followed by a M7.5 aftershock about 60 miles away just nine hours later. Aftershocks don't always occur on the same fault

---

[53] https://www.usgs.gov/faqs/what-difference-between-Earthquake-early-warning-Earthquake-forecasts-Earthquake-probabilities

as the mainshock, they only need to be close to its epicenter and occur after to be considered an aftershock. It's worth noting that the M7.5 aftershock did not lower the chance that another large Earthquake could still occur. Although the likelihood of future large aftershocks decreases over time, there always remains a small chance one will happen even months later.[54]

Fig. 3.2: Earthquake Probability

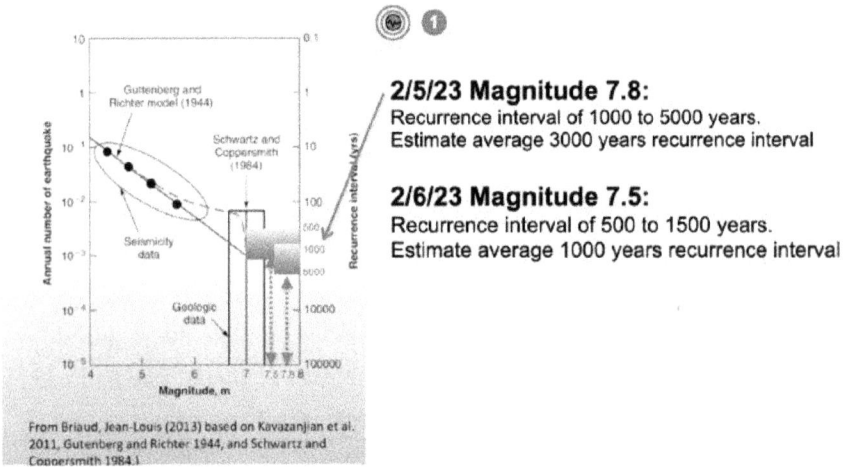

2/5/23 Magnitude 7.8:
Recurrence interval of 1000 to 5000 years.
Estimate average 3000 years recurrence interval

2/6/23 Magnitude 7.5:
Recurrence interval of 500 to 1500 years.
Estimate average 1000 years recurrence interval

From Briaud, Jean-Louis (2013) based on Kavazanjian et al. 2011, Gutenberg and Richter 1944, and Schwartz and Coppersmith 1984.)

(source: Soil Mechanics and Engineering Geology, Youtube)[55]

To estimate the Earthquake probability, Geo Engineering and Science, references two papers:

- Guttenberg and Richter model (1944)[56] for Magnitudes 6.x and under.

---

[54] https://www.usgs.gov/news/featured-story/m78-and-m75-kahramanmaras-Earthquake-sequence-near-nurdagi-turkey-turkiye

[55] GeoEngineeringandScience. (2023). How to Estimate Earthquake Probability and Recurrence Time. youtube.com/watch?v=UEi8cwrX2Vw

[56] GUTENBERG and C. F. RICHTER. (1944). Frequency of Earthquakes in California. BULLETIN OF TI-IE SEISMOLOGICAL SOCIETY OF AMERICA. https://core.ac.uk/download/pdf/216194157.pdf

- Schwartz and Coppersmith (1984)[57] for Magnitudes 7 and over.

See the graph representing both approaches to Earthquake probability estimation. Highlighted in red are the Magnitude 7.8 and 7.5 probability ranges.

Magnitude 7.8 Pazarcik = Probability 1/3000

AS USGS noted above "About **one in every 20 large-magnitude Earthquakes** will have a similar-sized aftershock". There were many aftershocks, but the probability of a similar-sized aftershock of a large-magnitude Earthquake, the following day of 7.5, should be factored into this equation at 1 out of every 20 large-magnitude Earthquakes.

Similar-sized aftershock for large-magnitude Earthquakes = Probability 1/20

Magnitude 7.5 Elbistan = Probability 1/1000

So assuming these are independent events, let's calculate this as a compounded probability of **independent events** (Note: reference Khan Academy to check my approach and thinking).

Independent Events:

1/3000 x 1/1000 = 1/3,000,000 = 1/3M

If however the 2nd M 7.5 was **not** an independent event, but was related and caused by the first M 7.8, then it was a significantly large aftershock and a probability of 1/20 is used. These **conditional events** would be calculated using the following formula.

Conditional Events: 1/3000 x 1/20 = 1/60,000 = 1/60k

3.3 Summarizing Probability and Proximity

Therefore our estimates show a 1/60k to 1/3M probability of these Earthquakes occurring. If the USGS is correct and the 2nd M7.5 Earthquake was a significantly large aftershock to the 1st M7.8, then the

[57] Schwartz, D.P. and Coppersmith, K.J. (1984) Fault behavior and characteristic Earthquakes-- examples from the Wasatch and San Andreas fault zones: Journal of Geophysical Research, v. 89, p. 5681-5698.

probability is 1/60k. If these two quakes were independent events, then the probability is 1/3M. These calculations are based upon the USGS and Soil Mechanics and Engineering Geology Earthquake probability numbers.

These calculations do not include the following "supernatural" aspects of the Earthquakes:

- **Probability of Geographical Proximity to the Seven Churches of Revelation** - This does not factor in the probability that the Earthquakes are in Turkey where the Apostle John writes the seven letters of Revelation from the Island Patmos to Ephesus, Smyrna, Pergamum, Thyatira, Sardis, Philadelphia, and Laodicea

  - Note: Elbistan, where the 2nd Earthquake occurred, is at the same latitude as Laodicea, Turkey and the Island of Patmos, Greece.

  - Israel is on the same fault line running south.

- **Probability of Temporal Proximity to the Fig Tree Generation** - This also doesn't factor in the probability that the 2023 Earthquakes fall in the middle of the Fig Tree Generation of 2018 to 2028 years.

  - 2023 is exactly 5 years after 2018.

  - 2023 is exactly 5 years before 2028.

What are the odds? I'm not sure how to calculate these supernatural probabilities. But in this series we will look at the independent events of the Earthquake, eclipses, meteor showers, etc… and the compounded result will be compelling enough.

As Dr. Roger Barrier writes in Crosswalk.com,

> It's my observation that some Christians, like my wife, have a very simple faith with which they seldom or ever doubt the reality of Jesus.

> I'm more like doubting Thomas. I want to see it to believe it. I do all sorts of studies and have experiences that help build

my faith because I tend to doubt. So, sharing the probability of Jesus Christ being real may be used in evangelism.

We never know when sharing this reality may be just what we need to help someone find Christ as their Lord and Savior.[58]

Understanding the reality of the fulfillment of Revelation Sixth Seal prophecies provides assurance that Christ is omnipotent and our faith should be strengthened that He is in control. These Earthquakes did occur and there is no doubt of their geographical and temporal significance.

Surveys reveal that about 80% of all Christians who come to Christ do so out of a sense of compassion. About 20% respond to commitment. A few respond to reason.

We never know when sharing this reality may be just what we need to help someone find Christ as their Lord and Savior.[59]

The statistics and probability exercise will be a pattern throughout each of these signs. We'll be alternating between the astronomical events with a subsequent chapter that will attempt to take the event and "show the work", break it down, and calculate whether this was a coincidence or not.

Disclaimer: I'm not a professional statistician, so forgive me for errors. My hope and prayer is this analysis will speak to the type of person who needs that extra proof to apologetics… where it is a mathematical impossibility that this is just coincidence, and can only point to God's divine plan, orchestrated in the Heavens.

3.4 Comet Path Connecting Heaven and Earth

The probability of Earthquakes is one aspect of understanding the rarity of these events; however, the following section has been added to include new research regarding the supernatural path of the comet. This research may provide a glimpse into a series of signs from Heaven that align with

---

[58] https://www.crosswalk.com/church/pastors-or-leadership/ask-roger/what-is-the-probability-of-the-reality-of-jesus-christ.html

[59] https://www.crosswalk.com/church/pastors-or-leadership/ask-roger/what-is-the-probability-of-the-reality-of-jesus-christ.html

what is occurring on Earth, while pulling prophetic words straight from Scripture.

Fig. 3.4.1: The Mazzaroth and the Green Comet

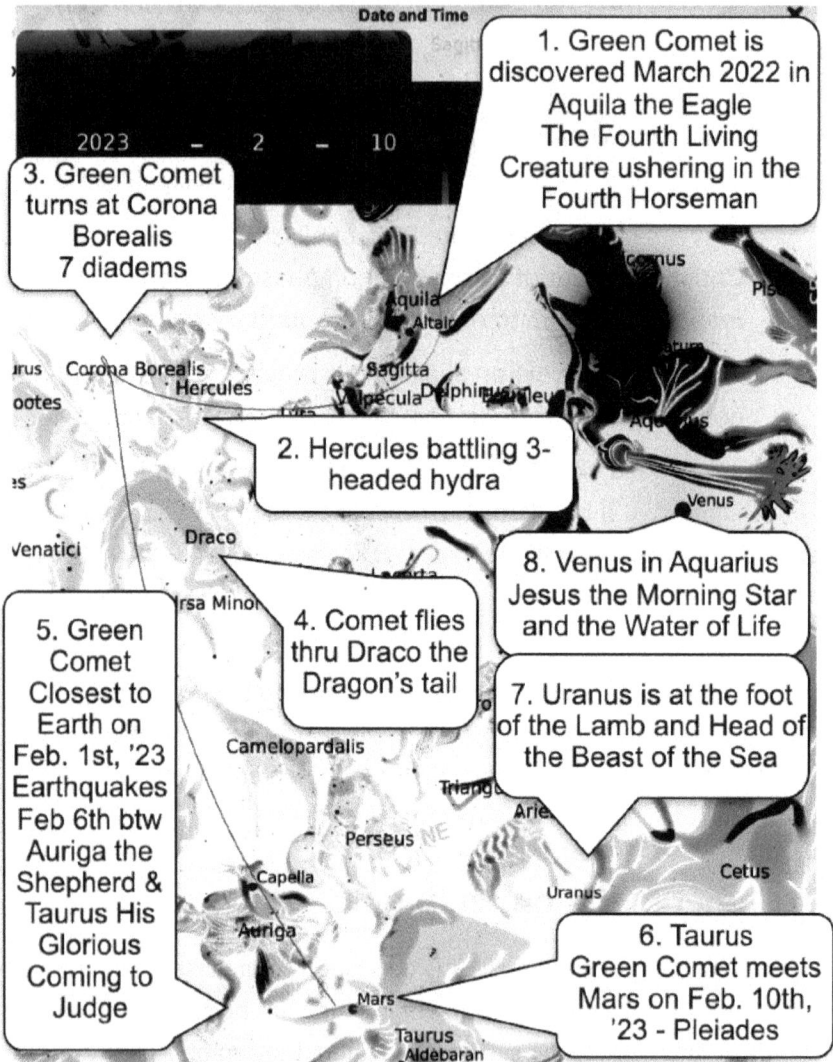

Let's summarize the path of the 2022 to 2023 Green Comet, or wandering star, that brings forth the Mazzaroth, as only Yahweh, the mighty God of Heaven and Earth, can do. See numbers called out in Fig. 3.6.

1. The Green Comet was discovered in March 2022 in Aquila, the Eagle, the Fourth Living Creature, ushering in the Fourth Horseman. See *The Signs of the Fourth Horsemen*.

2. The comet crosses Hercules, battling a 3-headed hydra

3. The comet makes a sharp turn at Corona Borealis, which is a crown made of 7-primary stars or diadems (Revelation 12:3). Note that this is one of two crowns, where the other is Corona Australis with 10-primary stars (Revelation 13:1).

4. The comet flies through Draco, the Dragon's tail, which parallels "⁴His tail swept down a third of the stars of Heaven and cast them to the Earth. Revelation 12:4". Later in this book, meteor showers from Draco the Dragon will be analyzed.

5. The Green Comet makes its closest approach to Earth on Feb. 1st, 2023. In the same week, Earthquakes break out on Feb 6th between Auriga, denoting the Shepherd & Taurus, denoting His Glorious Coming to Judge, researched by Ken Fleming. Is this a sign in Heaven and Earth?

6. In Taurus, the Green Comet meets Mars on the Horn of the Bull on Feb 10th, 2023. Death increased after the Great Earthquake in Turkey and Syria. Deaths also increase from wars and bioweapons. A "Green Comet" and the fourth horse in Revelation 6 is described as pale green (Greek *chloros*). Death is also the name of the Fourth Horseman on the pale green horse, followed by Hades. The conjunction of the comet with Mars is in Taurus, where the 7 stars of Pleiades, the "Congregation of the Judge", reside and are alluded to through Revelation, "The words of him who holds the seven stars in his right hand" Revelation 2:1.

7. Uranus is at the foot of the Lamb, Aries, and the Head of the Beast of the Sea, Cetus. Uranus in Greek is *ouranois* (Strong's Concordance 3772), which denotes Heaven, the abode of God.

8.   Venus is near the water pouring from the jar of Aquarius. Venus is symbolically known as Jesus the Morning Star, and Aquarius is symbolic of the Water of Life.

⁶ And he said to me, "It is done! I am the Alpha and the Omega, the beginning and the end. To the thirsty I will give from the spring of the **water of life** without payment. Revelation 21:6, ESV

The probability of two Earthquakes can be calculated; however, there is no way for us to calculate the probability of a Green Comet that has never before been seen, especially a comet that is discovered in Aquila, an "eagle in flight" (Revelation 4:7). The comet's path brings forth the Mazzaroth in so many ways.

The wandering green star traces signs in Heaven which is in temporal proximity to qEarthquakes on Earth. During this period between the comet's discovery in March 2022 and the Great Earthquake of February 6th, 2023, spiritual war escalates against those that follow the commands of Jesus Christ.

In the book, *The Signs of the Fourth Horseman*, the pale green horse is ushered in by an eagle, one of the Four Living creatures described in Revelation Chapter 4.

> ⁷ the first living creature like a lion, the second living creature like an ox, the third living creature with the face of a man, and the fourth living creature **like an eagle in flight**. Revelation 4:7, ESV[60]

Furthermore, the eagle ushers in the pale green horse with a rider named Death, which is in early 2022, shortly after the World Health Organization begins its mandates of injections across the Earth, heavily propagandized with "safe and effective" and "trust the science" programming. The great deception of sorcery is pushed over all nations and sudden deaths from a bioweapon begin to rise. Revelation Chapter 18 describes this sorcery in further detail.

---

[60] The Holy Bible: English Standard Version (Re 4:7). (2016). Crossway Bibles.

... and all nations were deceived by your **sorcery**.
Revelation 18:23b, ESV[61]

The Greek word for sorcery is *pharmekeia* (Strong's Concordance 5331) denoting medication, "pharmacy". While pharmakeus (Strong's Concordance 5332) can denote druggist, poisoner, and sorcerer.[62] There is death on Earth due to destructive Earthquakes and the deadly evil workings of a Beast System to inject mankind with a bioweapon.

In Revelation 12, besides the great sign that appears in Heaven of the woman, there is another sign of a great fiery red dragon, the serpent of old, Satan. The dragon's tail sweeps stars or meteors to Earth. In this book we will analyze the meteors of the Draconids.

Fig. 3.4.2: Comet, Corona, and Serpens

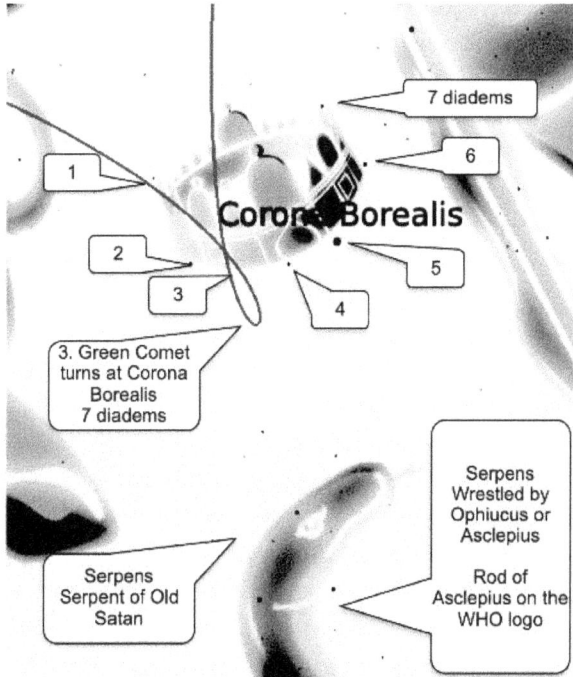

7 diadems

6

1

Coron Borealis

2

5

3

4

3. Green Comet turns at Corona Borealis 7 diadems

Serpens Wrestled by Ophiucus or Asclepius

Serpens Serpent of Old Satan

Rod of Asclepius on the WHO logo

(Source: Stellarium)

---

[61] The Holy Bible: English Standard Version (Re 18:23). (2016). Crossway Bibles.

[62] Strong, J. (2009). In A Concise Dictionary of the Words in the Greek Testament and The Hebrew Bible (Vol. 1, p. 75). Logos Bible Software.

On the dragon's head are seven diadems or crowns. The Green Comet makes a sharp turn at Corona Borealis which has 7 primary stars or diadems (See Fig. 3.7). The crown is just over the head of Serpens, the serpent which is being wrestled by Ophiucus, often also associated with Asclepius, the Greek god of medicine who used snake venom for healing. The Rod of Asclepius is what is found on the World Health Organization's (WHO) logo. Through the research found in *The Signs of the Fourth Horseman*, the United Nation's WHO on Earth parallel the Revelation 13 Beast of the Sea who is given authority by the serpent of old, Satan.

Fig. 3.4.3: Aquila, Serpens, and the Four Horsemen

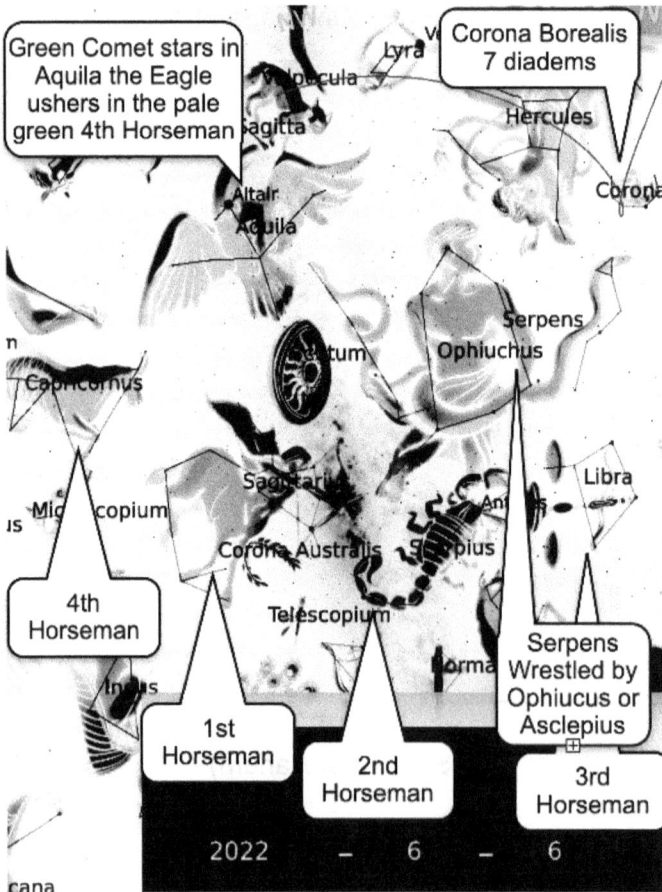

The Green Comet is shown in Fig 3.8, note the top-right corner of the screen shows the wandering star as it passes through Corona Borealis, this perspective of the Heavens reveals the full body of Serpens as it is entwined around Ophiucus (Asclepius god of medicine). The major constellations then arc along from left to right including Capricornus, Sagittarius, Scorpius, and Libra. These four constellations are detailed in *The Signs of the Four Horsemen.*

Probability is useful in analyzing Earthquakes, however, the path of the Green Comet through the Mazzaroth signs aligning with planets, Scripture, and Earthly events is mathematically an impossibility.

Let's close with an excerpt from The Signs of the Four Horseman closing Chapter,

> Here are some key takeaways. Do not fear the Four Horsemen for their ride is time bound and limited (Rev 6). Do not comply with the Beasts (Rev 13) who are thrown alive into the lake of fire (Rev 19:20). The dragon, Satan (Rev 12), will be chained for 1k years in the bottomless pit (Rev 20). The Beasts and Satan know their time is short, for the end of the age is near, and the judgements on Earth, mirrored by great signs in Heaven, are meant to call God's people to look up and repent.
>
> The Heavens proclaim His glory like a great clock in the universe. The Four Creatures and Four Horsemen are faces of that clock, while the sun, moon, planets, and comets are hands of this great timepiece.
>
> Jesus has conquered Death. As believers in Jesus Christ, we have been given the authority to conquer and overcome the evil and spiritual wickedness around us. Put on the Full Armor of God and be battle ready.
>
> The one who conquers and who keeps my works until the end, to him I will give authority over the nations

Revelation 2:26, ESV[63]

Chapter 4. The Sun as Black as Sackcloth

- How could the sun be black as sackcloth?

- What does this sign cross over?

- What is the significance of Salem?

> Then God said, "Let there be lights in the expanse of the Heavens to separate the day from the night, and let them be for **signs** and for seasons and for days and years;
> Genesis 1:14 (NASB1995)

> "There will be **signs** in *sun* and *moon* and *stars*, and on the Earth dismay among nations, in perplexity at the roaring of the sea and the waves,
> Luke 21:25 (NASB1995)

> "and the **sun became black as sackcloth** *made* of hair,"
> Revelation 6:12b (NASB1995)

In Genesis 1, the Hebrew word for *sign* is *oth* which is from *avah* (mark):

- *oth*: a sign; Original Word:אוֹת

- *avah*: to sign, mark, describe with a mark; Original Word: אָוָה

There are two upcoming solar eclipses: October 14th, 2023 is an annular solar eclipse:

---

63 The Holy Bible: English Standard Version (Re 2:26). (2016). Crossway Bibles.

An annular solar eclipse happens when the moon covers the sun's center, leaving the sun's visible outer edges to form a "ring of fire"[64]

This type of solar eclipse is not "black as sackcloth". However the total solar eclipse on April 8th, 2024 will be "black as sackcloth" in the path of totality.

Total solar eclipses happen when the new moon comes between the sun and Earth and casts the **darkest part of its shadow**, the umbra, on Earth.[65]

Is this God's mark, *avah*, which is when the sun will be as "black as sackcloth made of hair"? This will occur just over one year from the Earthquake in Turkey. A blink of an eye for God.

4.1 Let's review the Signs

"Part 1: Revelation 6: Sixth Seal Analysis - Are the Signs of Revelation being Unveiled?" In 2nd Peter 3:8, "But do not let this one fact escape your notice, beloved, that with the Lord one day is like a thousand years, and a thousand years like one day." Is the Lord letting us know that a few years in man's timeline is relatively brief in God's eyes? If yes, then the sequence of events in the Sixth Seal of Revelation 6 may be spread out over a few years in man's timeline which is a few minutes in God's timeline.

In this article, two total solar eclipses will be analyzed from 2017 and 2024, separated by 7 years, in relatively close temporal proximity to the Fig Tree Parable...

"Part 2: The Fig Tree Parable - What are the Interpretations? Is it a sign?" In the Fig Tree Parable, scholars believe the fig tree symbolizes Israel. The nation of Israel is established in 1948. A lifespan is 70 to 80 years (Psalm 90:10). Adding 70 and 80 years to 1948 results in a window

---

[64] https://www.timeanddate.com/eclipse/annular-solar-eclipse.html

[65] https://www.timeanddate.com/eclipse/total-solar-eclipse.html

of time between 2018 to 2028, respectively. This gives us a "high watch" period of 10 years for signs. 2018 is the the 70th anniversary of Israel as a nation where Israel has blossomed in the desert as the fig tree with its prosperity in natural resources, banking, and high-tech business accomplishments.

In the Synoptic Gospels it states "this generation will not pass away until all these things take place" (Mark 13:30, Matthew 24:34, Luke 21:32). The August 21, 2017 Total Solar Eclipse precedes the Revelation 12 September 23rd, 2017 sign of the woman clothed with the sun with with moon at her feet and 12 stars above her head as she gave birth, which precedes the 2018 window of the Fig Tree Parable. In 2017, Jerusalem, the *City of God*, is recognized as the the capitol of Israel by the United States under the Trump administration. Israel throws a huge celebration in 2018 to celebrate 70 years as a nation and there was rejoicing in the streets of Jerusalem and a dedication to the opening of the U.S. Embassy.

"Part 3: Over 57,000 deaths, was the Earthquake in Turkey and Syria a Sign?" In 2023, halfway between 2018 and 2028 (bookended by the Fig Tree Parable), the 4th largest Earthquake in the 21st century ranked by death toll, hits Southern Turkey and Northern Syria within geographical proximity of Israel. The explosive energy was equated to the eruption of Mount St. Helen.

Turkey is the biblical location of the 7 churches, where the last living Apostle John, the apostle that was loved by Jesus, His first cousin, who took care of His mother Mary, the apostle who wrote the Book of John that declares Jesus as God, uniquely different from the other Synoptic Gospels (i.e.: Matthew, Mark, and Luke) giving us insights to Jesus. John was banished to the island Patmos off the coast of Turkey where he wrote the seven letters of Revelation (i.e.: Ephesus, Smyrna, Pergamum, Thyatira, Sardis, Philadelphia, and Laodicea) through the inspiration of Jesus Christ.

In the early 1900's, the Ottoman Empire, persecuted Christians through massive genocides (i.e.: Armenian Genocide) and they were forced from the land. Today only 0.2% of the total population of Turkey are Christians.

One year after the 2023 Earthquake, a brief moment on God's timeline, another total solar eclipse will pass through the United States, turning the sun black as sackcloth. However, this total solar eclipse is in North America and not over Israel. Is there any relationship between North America and Israel in this sign? Let's look at a certain pattern that was noticed by Christians in the United States…

4.2 Overlapping Total Solar Eclipses

Here is a 2017 excerpt from a local paper where the two total solar eclipses will overlap

> CARBONDALE, IL – On Monday, August 21, 2017, the United States will experience a Total Solar Eclipse, the first one to cross the entire country in 99 years. The "Great American Eclipse" as it is being called, will reach its point of greatest duration just south of Carbondale, IL. The region won't have to wait long for another chance to be at the center of another total solar eclipse. There is a second eclipse on April 8, 2024, that will cross from Mexico to Maine. And you guessed it; the path of that eclipse will be right over Carbondale.
>
> This will be the first coast to coast total eclipse of the sun in the U.S. in 99 years.
> It will be the first total eclipse in the lower 48 states in 38 years.
>
> This will be followed by another in 2024 that will be visible in 13 states.[66]

Approximately, a 1+ hour drive north of Carbondale, IL is Salem, IL. *Salem* is the ancient name of *Jerusalem*. "OK but that's just one small town, no big deal right?"

_____

[66] https://www.wlky.com/article/cities-that-will-have-a-total-solar-eclipse-in-2017-and-2024/10378429#

4.3 The Seven Salems

Jerusalem c2000BC was known as *Salem* (See Genesis 14).

Salem, or Shalem, which is also the name of the God whose worship was centered in the city. The full name of this God was "God Most High, Creator of Heaven and Earth" since He was the God of creation.[67]

Chrisify, a 2017 blog, posted The Seven Salems of the Great 2017 Eclipse - Coincidence? on August, 13, 2017 with the following amazing image.[68] "The Seven Salems" went viral as the path of totality carved a path across the United States.

But wait, are there more Salems? After some research on the 2024 total solar eclipse there seems to be many more Salems within the path of both eclipses. Some are not dead center in the "path of totality", but fairly close. There are a couple Salem townships (in PA and ME), a Salem lake in VT, a Salem cemetery in WY, and even a Salem town in New Brunswick, Canada. NOTE: Not included is the infamous Salem, MA where the witch trials were held. Salem, MA was not included because it did not fall in the total solar eclipse path of totality. All together there are at least 19 Salems. Not the nice alliteration of "Seven Salems", or God's perfect number 7, but 19 seems much much more than coincidence and who can question the omnipotence of our God.

4.4 But Why Salem? What is the Significance?

Honestly only God knows and only time will tell what the significance of all the Salems in the path of these two total solar eclipses are, but it seems more than coincidence given the:

(1) **Close Temporal Proximity** to the Fig Tree Parable of Israel from 2018 to 2028, Revelation 12 signs of 2017, and the timing of the Earthquakes in Turkey and Syria.

---

[67] https://www.generationword.com/jerusalem101/16-salem-jebus.html

[68] http://blog.chrisify.com/2017/08/the-seven-salems-of-eclipse-coincidence.html

(2) **Geographical Proximity** between both total solar eclipses crossing ~19 Salems, and furthermore, at least by name, associated to the *City of God, Jerusalem.*

(3) **Biblical Significance** - "Salem, or Shalem, is the name of the God whose worship was centered in the City of God, Jerusalem. The full name of God:"God Most High, Creator of Heaven and Earth" since **He is the God of creation.** From Genesis, using the Amplified Bible:

> [18] Melchizedek king of **Salem (ancient Jerusalem)** brought out bread and wine [for them]; he was the priest of God Most High. [19]And Melchizedek blessed Abram and said, "Blessed (joyful, favored) be Abram by God Most High, Creator *and* Possessor of Heaven and Earth; [20] And blessed, praised, *and* glorified be God Most High, Who has given your enemies into your hand." Genesis 14:18-20, AMP

In Hebrew, Shalem denotes "peaceful".[69] Peaceful - 19x's.

In closing,

- How could the sun be black as sackcloth?

    - When one experiences a solar eclipse from Earth, sunlight filters in from the edges on the horizon

- What does this sign cross over?

    - The first solar eclipse in 2017 crosses over 7 Salems.

- What is the significance of Salem?

    - Salem is the ancient name of Jerusalem.

---

[69] https://biblehub.com/hebrew/8004.htm

Chapter 5. Solar Eclipses Crossing Crosses

On April 4th, 2023, the previous article was posted revealing 19 Salems crossed in the path of the two total solar eclipses (2017 and 2024).

- August 21st, 2017 Great Solar Eclipse travels from Salem, OR to Salem, SC

- April 8th, 2024 Great Solar Eclipse travels from Salem, TX to Salem, NB (Canada)

Updated 2025, this article has been supplemented with research from *The Signs of Jonah*, regarding a total of three solar eclipses and two crosses at the intersections.

The August 21st, 2017 solar eclipse is followed by an annular solar eclipse on October 14th, 2023 which traverses the Great National Parks of the Western States of the United States.

5.1 Another Salem

A new Salem found by "A lively hope", a Youtuber, who made the following video reveals something pretty amazing when you zoom down to the exact intersection of the two solar eclipses. (Source: Youtube, A Lively Hope, Intersection of 2017 & 2024 Total Solar Eclipses. Coincidence?)[70]

Key points from video detailed path of the two solar eclipses. These paths can be plotted using an online tool by Xavier M. Jubier. See the screenshot below of the path of the two solar eclipses as they traverse North America.[71]

---

[70] A Lively Hope. (2019). [Video] Intersection of 2017 & 2024 Total Solar Eclipses. Coincidence?. https://www.youtube.com/watch?v=zA3EDKAHRN0

[71] https://biblehub.com/hebrew/8004.htm

The paths of totality will cross over Makanda, Illinois, known as the "Star of Egypt". When zooming in on the exact intersection it was discovered that within 500 to 600 meters southeast there is a *Salem Road*, thus adding to our total count from 19 to **20 Salems**.

Among the foothills of the Ozark Mountain range that stretch into Union County and southern Illinois, rises a beacon, a monument of peace, faith, charity, and of hope.

Towering above the landscape at over 111 feet, and **visible for over 7,500 square miles,** this is the Bald Knob Cross of Peace – one of the largest crosses in the United States.

Bald Knob Cross is situated in the Shawnee National Forest near the small town of Alto Pass, Illinois. BK Mountain itself towers 1000 feet above sea level.

But how did a mountaintop in rural southern Illinois become first the site of an annual sunrise service, and later the location of an 111 foot cross? The story begins in the spring of 1936.[72] So this huge cross was built far before the total solar eclipses.

5.2 Cross #1: The Cross of Peace

In 1963 the Bald Knob "Cross of Peace" was built on a mountain top and it is within the path of totality for both the August 21st, 2017, and the April 8th, 2024 total solar eclipses. The 2 total solar eclipses also crossed over ~20 Salems, the ancient name of Jerusalem. Salem which also means "peace" in Hebrew. The Bald Knob "Cross of Peace" is 111 feet high: The number 111 is spiritually significant because it represents God's unity, authority, and revelations. If you see the number 111, pray. God may be trying to reveal or relay an important message. 111 is sometimes used to express the Holy Trinity: the Father, the Son, and the Holy Spirit.

---

[72] https://www.baldknobcross.com/about-us/

Fig. 5.2: The Cross of Peace

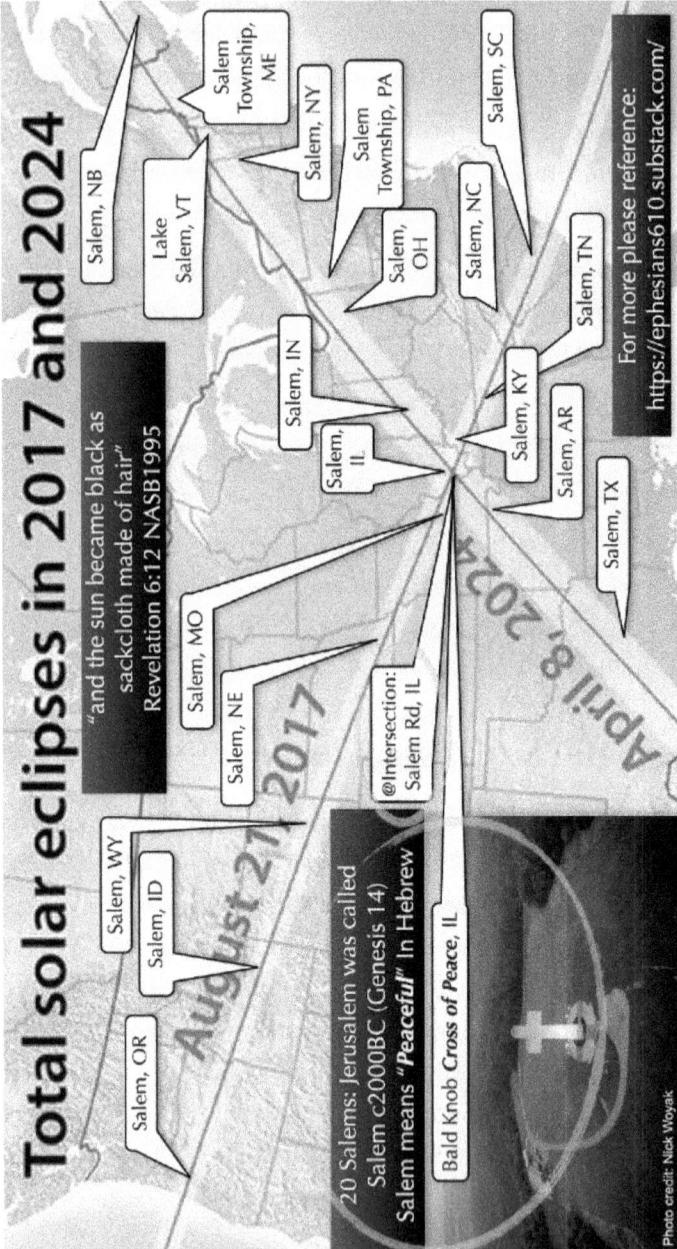

Psalm is the only book in the Bible with 111 chapters. (Psalm 111)[73]

> Praise the Lord! I will give thanks to the Lord with my whole heart, in the company of the upright, in the congregation. Psalm 111:1, ESV[74]

We give thanks for Jesus Christ and "The Strength of His Blood Covenant" which He has made known to all the nations.

5.3 Cross #2: The Empty Cross

The following press release was published in 2010,

> KERRVILLE, TX, July 28, 2010 -- Tuesday a two-million-dollar, 70-ton, 77'7" red-brown contemporary sculpture named The Empty Cross was erected by The Coming King Foundation (TCKF) overlooking Interstate 10, half-way between the Atlantic and Pacific Oceans, on the transcontinental highway that connects California and Florida.[75]

> God Himself is pointing the world to "The Empty Cross" at The Coming King Sculpture Prayer Garden in Kerrville, Texas, halfway between the Atlantic and Pacific Oceans at the same latitude as ISRAEL. The Annular Eclipse (10/14/23) and the Total Eclipse (4/8/24) forever point to Jesus Christ!

> The unique hollow cross symbolizes the Resurrection of Jesus Christ. The "walk-in" cross sculpture is being displayed at the top of a 1,930' hill, at the end of a 100 yard long cross-shaped Garden. The Garden when completed, will display 77 Biblical scriptures on 16" etched ceramic tiles in multiple languages. According to Max and Sherry Greiner, God "called" them on December 9, 2001 to build a "last days,

---

[73] https://www.wikihow.com/Bible-Meaning-of-111

[74] The Holy Bible: English Standard Version (Ps 111:1). (2016). Crossway Bibles.

[75] https://www.24-7pressrelease.com/press-release/163097/777-kerrville-cross-raised-on-ih-10-ending-9-year-epic-struggle

outdoor tabernacle" as a way of sharing the love of Jesus Christ with the world.[76]

Fig. 5.3: The Empty Cross

(Source: The Coming King Foundation, Kerrville, TX)[77]

Like the Cross of Peace at 111 ft, there is symbolism with The Empty Cross at 77'7". According to Crosswalk.com, the number 777 means the perfection of the Trinity (God the Father, Jesus Christ the Son, and the Holy Spirit), according to the number's use in Hebrew tradition.[78] *Nelson's New Illustrated Bible Dictionary* notes that 7 is a sacred number to the ancient Hebrew people and used often in the Bible to symbolize perfection, fullness, abundance, rest, and completion[79] (e.g.: 7 Days of Creation). In

---

[76] Ibid.

[77] https://thecomingkingfoundation.org/watch-eclipses-in-kerrville/

[78] Hopler, W. (2022). What Is the Meaning of 777 in the Bible?. Crosswalk.com. https://www.crosswalk.com/faith/bible-study/what-is-the-meaning-of-777-in-the-bible.html

[79] Youngblood, R. (1995). Nelson's New Illustrated Bible Dictionary.

Revelation there are 7 angels, 7 stars, 7 lamp stands, and 7 letters to the 7 churches. There are the judgements of the 7 seals, 7 trumpets, and 7 bowls (Revelation 5, 8, and 15).

> **16** In His right hand He held **seven stars**, and out of His mouth came a sharp two-edged sword; and His face was like the sun shining in its strength.
>
> Revelation 1:16, NASB1995

In addition, there is a star cluster that is mentioned in the Bible that is made up of a cluster of **7 primary stars, the Pleiades** (Job 9:9, 38:31). Pleiades is interpreted by Ken Fleming as the "Congregation of the Judge" denoting "Christ the Judge, His Glorious Coming".[80],[81]

5.4 The Three Solar Eclipses Cross 2 out of ~40 Crosses

The three 2017, 2023, and 2024 solar eclipses have been plotted with the locations of the "Tallest Crosses in the World". Approximately 40 of those crosses reside in the United States, reflecting the Judeo-Christian values of the people in this great nation. Two of those crosses covered in this article fall in the April 8th, 2024 path of totality where the sun is black as sackcloth. Those two crosses happen to be: The Bald Knob Cross of Peace in Alto Pass, IL, and The Empty Cross at The Coming King Sculpture Prayer Garden in Kerrville, TX. Salem is the ancient name of Jerusalem. Salem means "Peaceful" in Hebrew. Shalom Shalom in Hebrew is used as a double blessing. What are the odds? In the next chapter, let's analyze the odds.

---

[80] Law. E. E. (2023). Constellation Pleiades: The Seven Stars & Seven Angels. https://ephesians610.substack.com/p/constellation-pleiades-the-seven

[81] Fleming, K. C. (1981). *God's Voice in the Stars*, Loizeaux Brothers, Neptune, New Jersey.

Chapter 6. Probability of the Signs of Jonah?

2025 Update: This chapter has been supplemented with not just a probability calculation of 2 solar eclipses but also a look at the Mazzaroth signs highlighted by all three solar eclipses from *The Signs of Jonah*.

What is the probability of two independent solar eclipses with the Earthquake and aftershock?

Answer:
1 in 9,600,000,000
1 in 9.6e9, 9.6 Billion

Show work below

6.1 Probability of an Eclipse casting a Shadow on Salems?

The statistical results of 1 out of 9.6 Billion (above) primarily look at the astronomical and geological probability of these events occurring.

It does not take into account the "supernatural Salems". Salem being the ancient name of Jerusalem the City of God. <u>Salem meaning "peaceful" in Hebrew and the probability of a "Cross of Peace" at the center of the X that marks the center</u>. Salem is also "Shalom, Shalom" or a "double blessing"[82].

What are the odds?

Geotargit.com below notes there are 36 Salem's in America.

_____

[82] https://hebrewrootsmom.com/explaining-the-chosen-season-2-episode-2-i-saw-you/

Fig. 6.1: Salem's in America

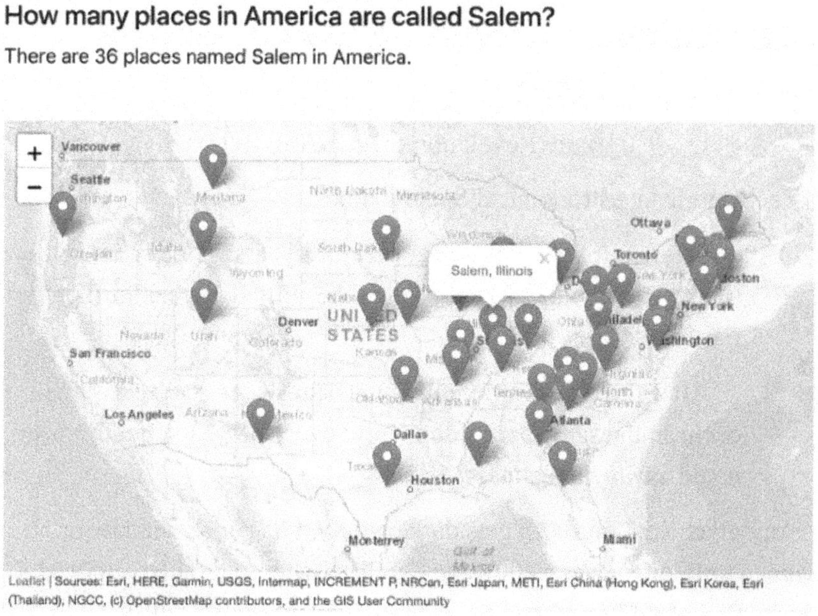
How many places in America are called Salem?
There are 36 places named Salem in America.
Vancouver
Seattle
Ottawa
Toronto
Boston
New York
Washington
Salem, Illinois
Denver
UNITED STATES
San Francisco
Los Angeles
Dallas
Houston
Atlanta
Monterrey
Miami
Leaflet | Sources: Esri, HERE, Garmin, USGS, Intermap, INCREMENT P, NRCan, Esri Japan, METI, Esri China (Hong Kong), Esri Korea, Esri (Thailand), NGCC, (c) OpenStreetMap contributors, and the GIS User Community

(source: geotargit.com)[83]

And below simplemaps.com notes there are ~109,000 cities and towns in the U.S. (source: simplemaps.com)[84]

The probability of drawing a line and hitting a town or city of Salem is therefore 36 out of 109,000.

Probability of 1 Salem: 36/109,000 = 1/3028

Probability of 2 Salems: 1/3028 x 1/3028 = ~1/9.2M

Probability of 3 Salems: 1/3028^3 = 1/27,763,077,952

Probability of 10 Salems: 1/3028^5 = 1/6.5e34

Probability of 20 Salems: 1/3028^20 = 1/4.2e69 = one in four duovigintillion two hundred unvigintillion

---

[83] https://geotargit.com/citiespercountry.php?qcountry_code=US&qcity=Salem

[84] https://simplemaps.com/data/us-cities#:~:text=Up%2Dto%2Ddate%3A%20Data,and%20the%20US%20Virgin%20Islands.

Ponder the magnitude of this impossibility. God can do the impossible.

6.2 Probability of 2 Total Solar Eclipses

Let's look at the astronomical probability of the <u>sun became black as sackcloth made of hair</u> (Revelation 6:12, NASB 1995).

The American Astronomical Society notes:

- Solar eclipse cycles repeat every 18 years, 11 days, and 8 hours (<u>Saros cycle</u>) but each eclipse will be shifted by one third of the Earth's rotation.

- After three cycles (exigimos), a nearly identical eclipse will occur in the same part of the world every 54 years, but these are noted as *partial* eclipses.[85]

Any given spot on Earth gets darkened by the Moon's shadow on average **only once every 400 years**, so in that sense totality is indeed rare.[86] Probability of a Total Solar Eclipse is approximately 1 out of 400.

To calculate the probability of two independent total solar eclipses:

Estimated Probability of 2 Independent Total Solar Eclipses: 1/400 x 1/400 = 1/160,000

Now let's look at both the Earthquake, aftershock and two solar eclipses:

Estimated Probability of 2 Independent Total Solar Eclipses, the M7.8 Earthquake and the M7.5 Aftershock

1/60k x 1/160k = 1/9.6e9 = 1 out of 9.6 Billion

---

[85] https://eclipse.gsfc.nasa.gov/SEsaros/SEsaros.html

[86] American Astronomical Society. (2023). How & Why Solar Eclipses Happen. eclipse.aas.org. https://eclipse.aas.org/eclipse-america/how-why

6.3 The Signs of Jonah?

Fig 6.3.1 2017, 2023, 2024 Solar Eclipses

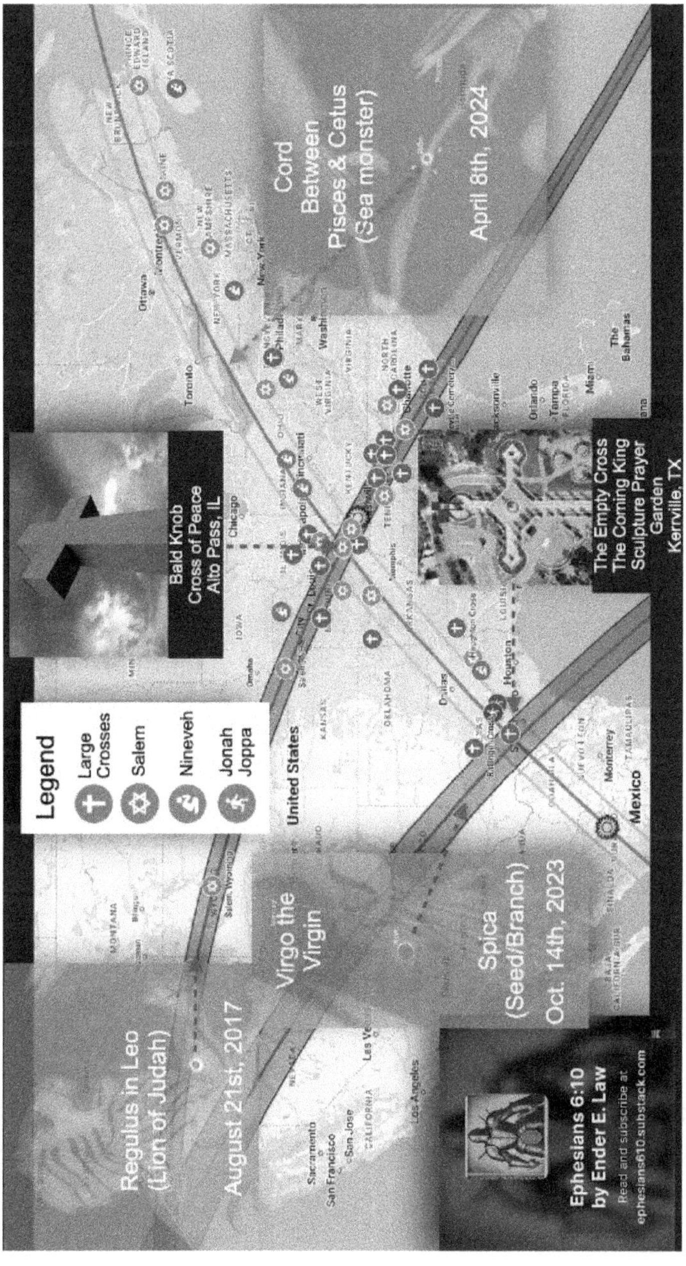

- What will the Great Solar eclipses do in our time?

- Are they just an astronomical alignment or is there more divine intervention?

- Does God seek repentance from this land?

> **14** and My people who are called by My name humble themselves and pray and seek My face and turn from their wicked ways, then I will hear from Heaven, will forgive their sin and will heal their land.

> 2 Chronicles 7:14, NASB1995

In researching the meaning behind these solar eclipses, more was uncovered that included additional towns and crosses that were traversed by not only 2 total solar eclipses, but also a third annular solar eclipse. Therefore there are three solar eclipses in 2017, 2023, and 2024 across North America.

The towns included Nineveh, Joppa, and Jonah. These seemed to harken back to the story of Jonah. This scholarly research led to a third book, *The Signs of Jonah* in the Signs Series, by Ender E. Law[87]. So often watchmen were looking at the path of the solar eclipses, but few were watching the placement of the solar eclipses in the Mazzaroth.

When one steps back and looks up into the Heavens, a story board is highlighted by the sun and moon being eclipsed against the Mazzaroth. These signs are not just isolated to the eclipses, but they also highlight repeating Mazzaroth signs which span time to previous significant signs.

The August 21st, 2017 total solar eclipse is ~1 degree from Regulus the little king. It is awe inspiring for this is the same star that is crowned by Jupiter three times during and after the date of September 11th, 3 BC where there is an alignment in Virgo the Virgin and Leo the Lion. This date appears to be the actual birth of Jesus Christ, as analyzed in the second book in the series, *The Covenant Signs* and a future book, *The Signs of*

---

[87] Law, E. E. (2025). *The Signs of Jonah - An Investigation of the Solar Eclipses, the Mazzaroth, the Beast of the Sea, and the Alef Tav.* Ephesians610

Immanuel (~2026). Regulus, is interpreted as the little king, which seems appropriate for the birth of baby Jesus, the King of Kings.

Regulus is also the star which aligns with Mercury, Mars, and Venus on September 23rd, 2017, approximately one month after the August 21st, 2017 total solar eclipse. This alignment included Jupiter in the womb of Virgo for 9 months near the star Spica, the seed or branch, representing the Seed of the Woman and Jesus, the branch.

Fig 6.3.2 Aug. 21st, 2017 Total Solar Eclipse Regulus Conjunction

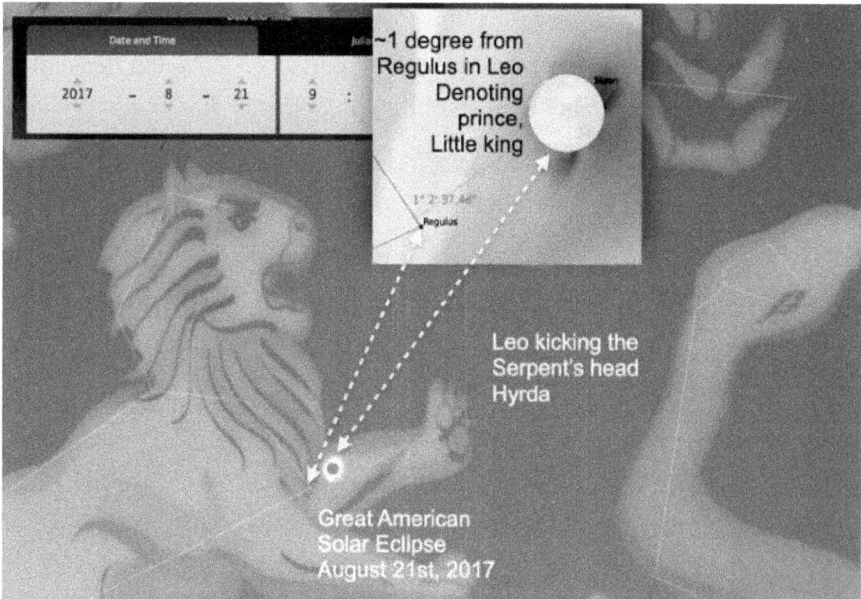

(Source: Stellarium)

The August 21st, 2017 solar eclipse is followed by an annular solar eclipse on October 14th, 2023 which traverses the Great National Parks of the Western States of the United States. This eclipse forms a ring of fire in the hand of the Virgin as she tightly holds the bundle of wheat or barley. The Virgin Mazzaroth sign includes the star Spica, the seed or branch. God is in control from the Protoevangelium (Genesis 3:15), since the fall in the Garden of Eden to the signs of Noah's Flood, the birth sign of Immanuel, and the great sign in Heaven of Revelation 12. The Seed of the Woman reoccurs as a celestial sign. The signs highlight the seed, the star

Spica, a theme warning watchmen of a "Seed War" (For more details please read *The Covenant Signs*). Satan will do what he can to destroy the temple of the Holy Spirit. We are created in the image of God and we must protect the seed from corruption.[88] We are the steward-masters of Creation.[89]

The last two eclipses fall near Regulus, the little king, and Spica, the seed of the woman. These two solar eclipses [2017 to 2023] and the Revelation 12 sign [2017] coincide with an unprecedented campaign of fear and control.[90] The third total solar eclipse on April 8th, 2024 falls squarely on a rope between Cetus, a sea monster, and Pisces. The picture in the Second Heavens is a celestial tug-of-war between Cetus, the Beast of the Sea, the Leviathan, and two fish pulling in opposite directions.[91]

The Leviathan in Hebrew is *Livyathan* (Strong's Concordance 3882)[92], which denotes "serpent", a sea monster or dragon.

God is speaking to Job in the following passage,

> Can you pull in *Leviathan* with a fishhook or tie down its tongue with a rope? Can you put a cord through its nose or pierce its jaw with a hook? Job 41:1-2, NASB1995

In closing, here is a timeline of the solar eclipse signs. The probability of three solar eclipses spanning 7 years across the continental United States which highlight the Gospel Story of the birth of Jesus Christ, to the Seed of the Woman, to the epic spiritual war between the Beast of the Sea and those that follow the commands of Jesus Christ seems mathematically

---

[88] Law, E. E. (2023). Satan causing man to play god in corrupting the seed? (Reference Transhumanism: Guard your Soul, Spirit, and DNA)

[89] Law, E. E. (2025). *The Signs of Jonah - An Investigation of the Solar Eclipses, the Mazzaroth, the Beast of the Sea, and the Alef Tav.* Ephesians610

[90] *(Reference: The Second Horseman and parallels to War (Part 1 of 2)). Signs of transhumanism? Satan causing man to play god in corrupting the seed? (Reference Transhumanism: Guard your Soul, Spirit, and DNA)*

[91] Law, E. E. (2025). *The Signs of Jonah - An Investigation of the Solar Eclipses, the Mazzaroth, the Beast of the Sea, and the Alef Tav.* Ephesians610

[92] https://biblehub.com/hebrew/3882.htm

impossible. However, the Sixth Seal Signs are being revealed to us in Heaven and on Earth.

Fig 6.3.3 October 14th, 2023 Annular Solar Eclipse near Spica

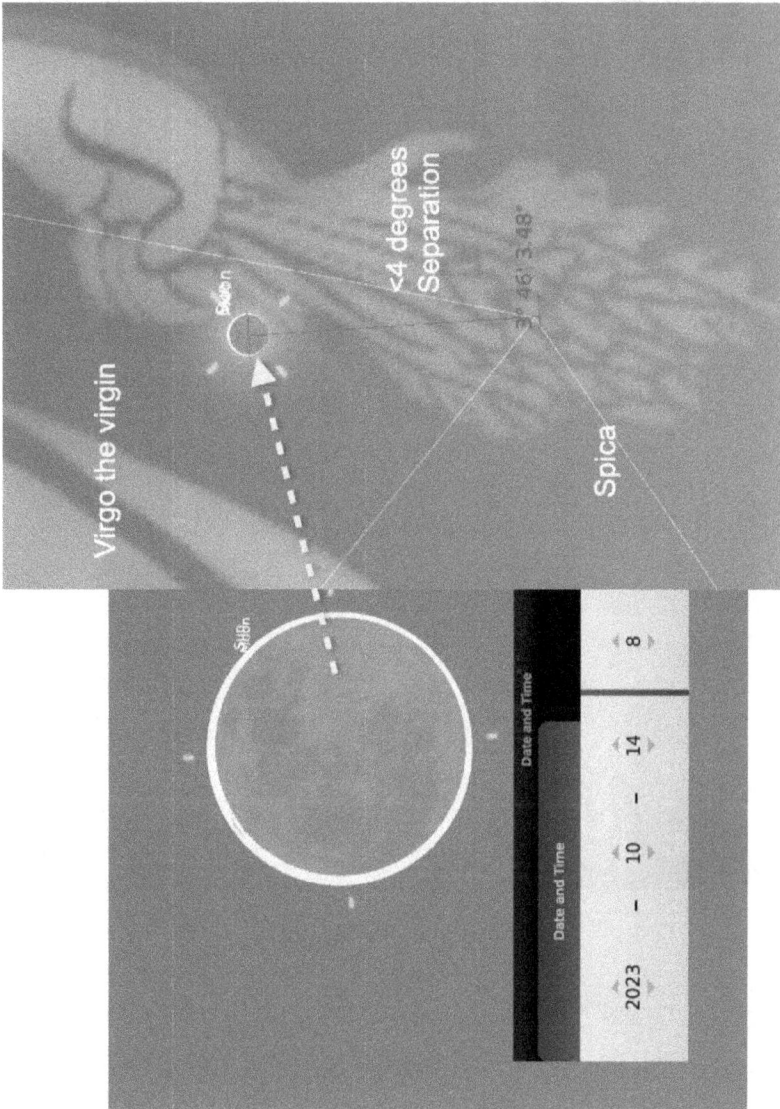

Fig 6.3.4 April 8th, 2024: Total Solar Eclipse btw Cetus and Pisces

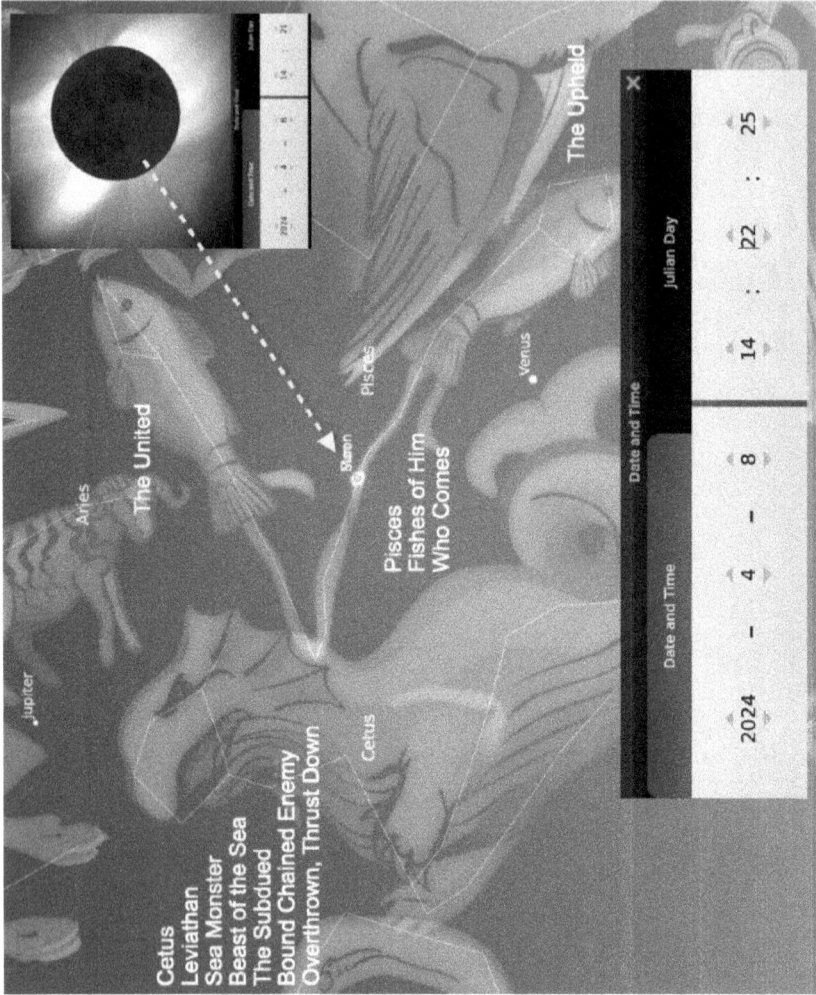

(Source: Stellarium)

Fig 6.4.5 Timeline: 2017, 2023, and 2024 Signs

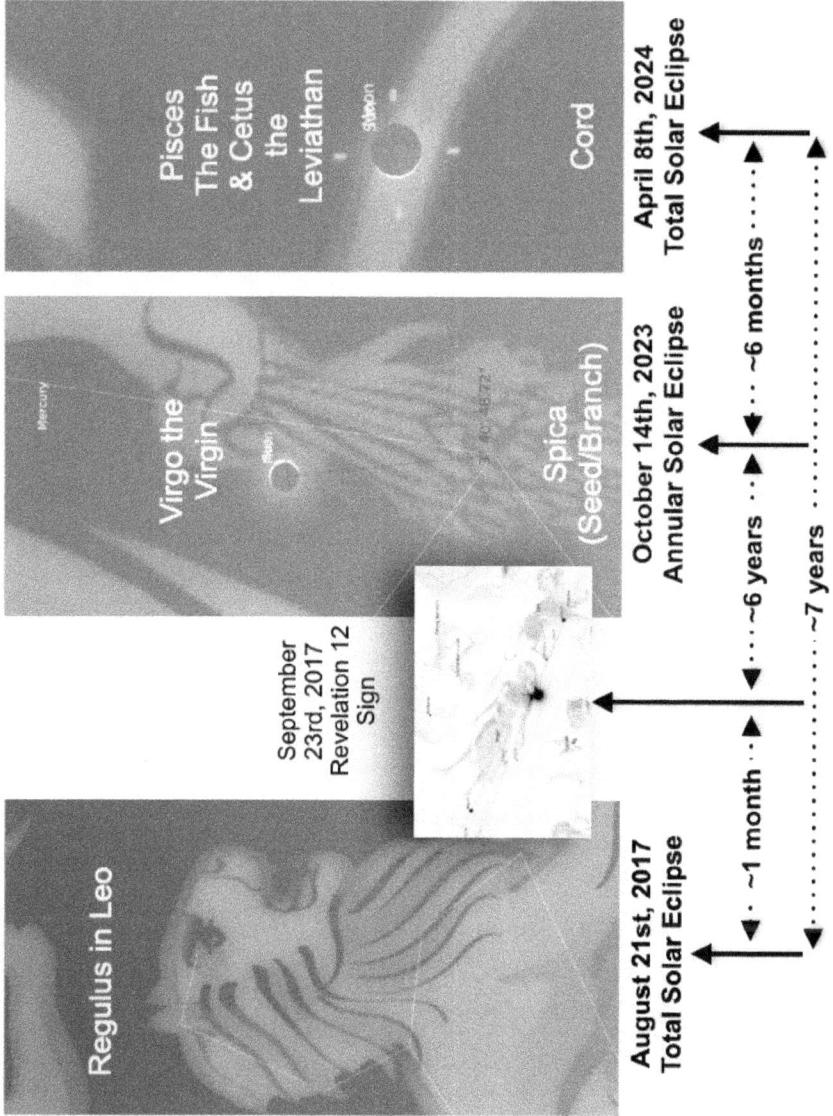

Let's continues with the blood moons.

Chapter 7. Are the Pair of Blood Moons a Sign?

This is a multi-part series, connecting-the-dots across different signs which are summarized in the following timeline.

Disclaimer:

• This analysis is a literal Futurist/Premillennial view of Bible Prophecy which is the eschatological belief that Jesus will return in the near future, therefore be on alert.

• My hope is we can all ponder the events that are unfolding and wonder at God's amazing plan.

• For the unbeliever and the denier, please look at this as a sequence of geological and astronomical events. These events just so happen to align with ancient scripture writings from 2000-2500 years ago.

Let's review Revelation 6:12-13:

> I looked when He broke the sixth seal, and
> there was a great Earthquake; and
> the sun became black as sackcloth made of hair, and
> the **whole moon became like blood;**
> and the stars of the sky fell to the Earth, as a fig tree casts its
> unripe figs when shaken by a great wind.
>
> Revelation 6:12-13, NASB1995

Fig. 7.0 "Signs of the Times" Timeline Review

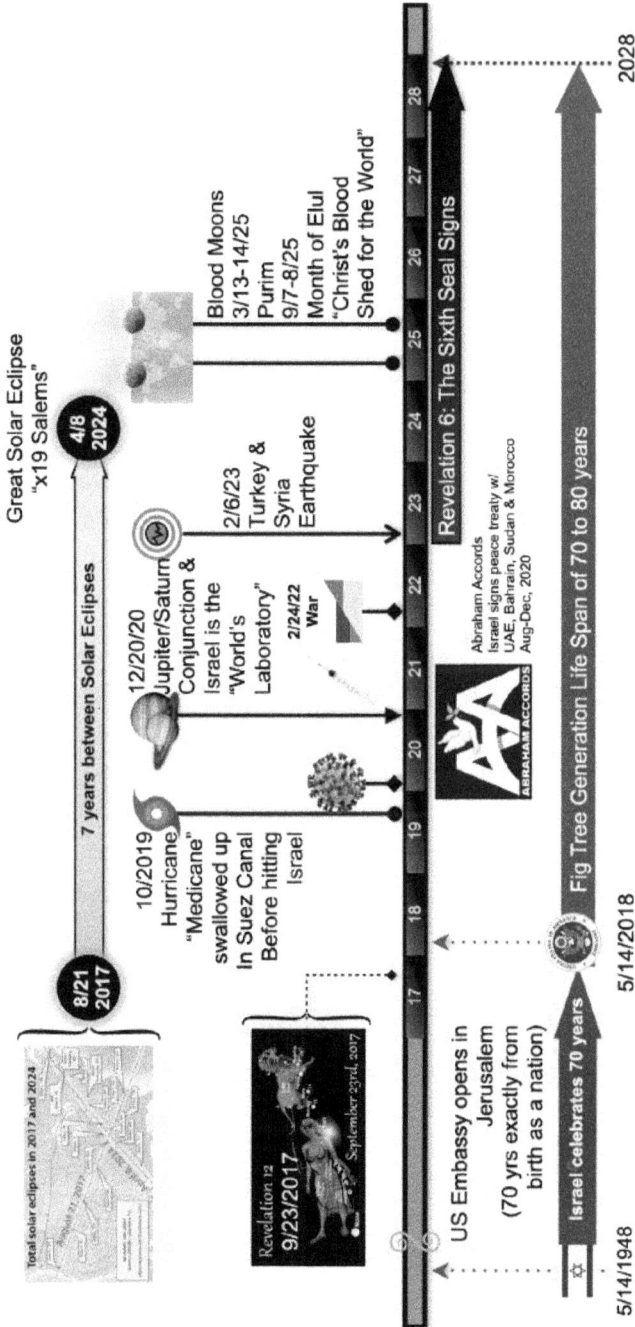

Great Solar Eclipse
"x19 Salems"

8/21 2017

4/8 2024

7 years between Solar Eclipses

Total solar eclipses in 2017 and 2024

10/2019
Hurricane "Medicane" swallowed up In Suez Canal Before hitting Israel

12/20/20
Jupiter/Saturn Conjunction & Israel is the "World's Laboratory"

2/24/22 War

2/6/23
Turkey & Syria Earthquake

Blood Moons
3/13-14/25
Purim
9/7-8/25
Month of Elul
"Christ's Blood Shed for the World"

Revelation 6: The Sixth Seal Signs

Abraham Accords
Israel signs peace treaty w/ UAE, Bahrain, Sudan & Morocco Aug-Dec, 2020

ABRAHAM ACCORDS

Revelation 12
9/23/2017
September 23rd, 2017

US Embassy opens in Jerusalem
(70 yrs exactly from birth as a nation)

5/14/2018

Israel celebrates 70 years

Fig Tree Generation Life Span of 70 to 80 years

5/14/1948

2028

73

Revelation 6: Sixth Seal Analysis - Are the Signs of Revelation being Unveiled?

Temporal Proximity: The following occur relatively close to each other: Revelation 12 sign in Heaven. September 23rd, 2017 there was a great sign in Heaven, the woman clothed with the sun, the moon at her feet, she was giving birth, and there were twelve stars above her head. Israel becomes a nation on 5/14/1948 and the Trump Administration opens the US Embassy in Jerusalem on 5/14/2018, exactly 70 years to the day. Again we see God's perfect number **7. Seven** years after 2018, the **70th** anniversary of Israel as a nation, are two blood moons in 2025 which this article will cover in detail. Two blood moons that seem to cast their blood red light on all the nations of the world.

Geographical Proximity: The following occurs relatively close to Israel or is associated with Jerusalem. August 21st, 2017 the first "Great American Solar Eclipse" crosses Seven Salems (the ancient name of Jerusalem), later that same year: November 29th, 2017 - TV: Israel expects Trump to recognize Jerusalem as Israel's capital within days (Times of Israel). December 17th, 2017 - U.N. Votes Overwhelmingly To Condemn U.S. Decision On Jerusalem. **Seven Years** (God's Perfect Number 7) from 2017 is 2024, the next "Great American Solar Eclipse" which will cross another 12 Salems for a total of at least 19 Salems. Jerusalem is the City of God, Salem also means "Peaceful" in Hebrew, and it is a double blessing when spoken as in "Shalom, Shalom".

7.1 The Fig Tree Parable - What are the Interpretations? Is it a sign?

- See the 70 to 80 years timeline from 1948 above (purple).

- In 2018, Israel celebrates its 70th anniversary as a nation.

- May 14th, 2018 - 'You have made history': Netanyahu hails Trump at Jerusalem embassy opening

32 "Now learn the parable from the fig tree [*Israel*]: when its branch has already become tender and puts forth its leaves [*Israel becomes a nation and prospers*], you know that summer is near; so, you too, when you see all these things, recognize that He is near, right at the door. Truly I say to you, this generation [*The 70 to 80 years lifespan of the generation born 1948*] will not pass away until all these things take place. Heaven and Earth will pass away, but My words will not pass away. Matthew 24:32-33, NASB1995

7.2 Was the Earthquake in Turkey and Syria a Sign?

- The 2/6/2023 Great Earthquake is shown on the timeline

- The "Fig Tree" symbolizes Israel while the "Olive Tree" symbolizes Syria. The border of Turkey and Syria is where an olive orchard was torn apart, the width of a football field and the new gorge has a depth up to 13 stories.

7.3 The Sun Became Black as Sackcloth

The 2 total solar eclipses are highlighted which cross North America in August 21st, 2017 and April 8th, 2024, approximately **7 years apart** (yellow). In total the two solar eclipses cross 19 Salems, the ancient name for Jerusalem, the City of God, but there is more. August 21st, 2017 - This is approximately 1 month before the Revelation 12 sign of the woman clothed with the sun. April 8th, 2024 - Timed ~7 years after the 2017 solar eclipse and a week after Easter on Marc h 31st, 2024.

7.4 The Moon Became Like Blood

The word *haima* is used to describe the *blood of Jesus, blood shed*, and *blood moon* such as in the following verses:

> The sun will be turned into darkness and the **moon into blood**, before the great and glorious day of the Lord shall come. Acts 2:20, NASB1995

The sun will be turned into darkness and the **moon into blood,** before the great and awesome day of the Lord comes. Joel 2:31, NASB1995

I looked when He broke the sixth seal, and there was a great Earthquake; and the sun became black as sackcloth made of hair, and the **whole moon became like blood**; Revelation 6:12, NASB1995

In addition to Acts 2:20, Joel 2:31, and Revelation 6:12, what other scriptures describe a possible "blood moon" or similar signs in the moon?

7.5 Additional Scripture Review:

In the Synoptic Gospels, Luke notes there will be signs in the moon, while Mark and Matthew describe the moon will not give its light.

"There will be signs (attesting miracles) in the sun and **moon** and stars; and on the Earth [there will be] distress *and* anguish among nations, in perplexity at the roaring *and* tossing of the sea and the waves. (Luke 21:25, AMP)

"But in those days, after [the suffering and distress of] that tribulation, THE SUN WILL BE DARKENED, AND **THE MOON WILL NOT GIVE ITS LIGHT** (Mark 13:24 AMP)

"Immediately after the tribulation of those days THE SUN WILL BE DARKENED, AND **THE MOON WILL NOT PROVIDE ITS LIGHT**, AND THE STARS WILL FALL from the sky, and the powers of the Heavens will be shaken. (Matthew 24:29 AMP)

How does the moon "not provide its light"? A Lunar Eclipse.

Fig 7.5.1 Path March 13-14, 2025 Lunar Eclipse

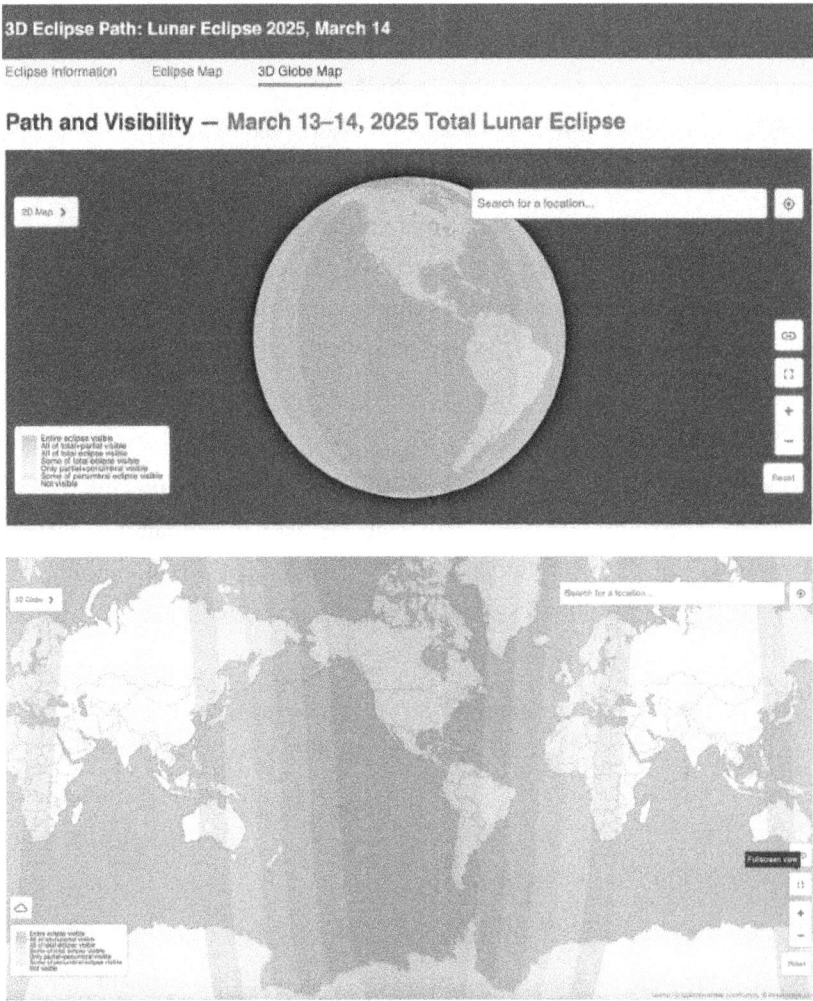

(source: **Time and Date**)[93]7.6 Between 2020 and 2029 there are 9 Total Lunar Eclipses.

---

[93] https://www.timeanddate.com/eclipse/globe/2025-march-14

Three have already passed in 2021 and 2023, where two eclipses cover oceans and one South America. There are no total lunar eclipses in 2023 or 2024. Another total eclipse appears in 2026, primarily over the ocean. There are three more total eclipses in 2029 that cover Asia, South America, Africa, and Europe, but none cover North America. This in itself could be significant but let's analyze 2025. In 2025 there are two total lunar eclipses which span major continents of the world. Let's take a look at these closer.[94]

Almost one year after the total solar eclipse of 2024, there will be a blood moon which will be visible across North and South America. The blood moon nearly casts a direct hit right over both continents. It's not a glancing red shadow, but a full deep blood red that will be visible across all nation states from Canada, the United States, Mexico, and all Latin American countries.

March 13-14, 2025 is also a Jewish holiday, Purim. Purim celebrates the deliverance of the Jewish people from the wicked Haman in the days of Queen Esther of Persia.[95] September 7-8th, 2025: The whole moon becomes like blood again. Notice the blood moon covers Asia, Australia, the Middle East, Europe, and Africa.

This period is also significant to Jews: **The Month of Elul - August 25 - September 22, 2025.** Elul is the 12th and final month in the Jewish calendar (the sixth month counting from Nisan). It is a month that connects the past year with the coming year—a time when we reflect on where we stand and where we should be going.

Every day of Elul we blow the shofar and recite special Psalms in anticipation of the High Holidays, Rosh Hashanah and Yom Kippur.[96] **Rosh Hashanah**

---

[94] https://www.timeanddate.com/eclipse/globe/2025-march-14

[95] https://www.chabad.org/holidays/default_cdo/year/2025/jewish/holidays-2025.htm

[96] https://www.chabad.org/holidays/JewishNewYear/template_cdo/aid/4685/jewish/Month-of-Elul.htm

- Begins sunset of Monday, September 22, 2025

- Ends nightfall of Wednesday, September 24, 2025

Fig 7.5.2 Path September 7-8, 2025 Lunar Eclipse

Path and Visibility — September 7–8, 2025 Total Lunar Eclipse

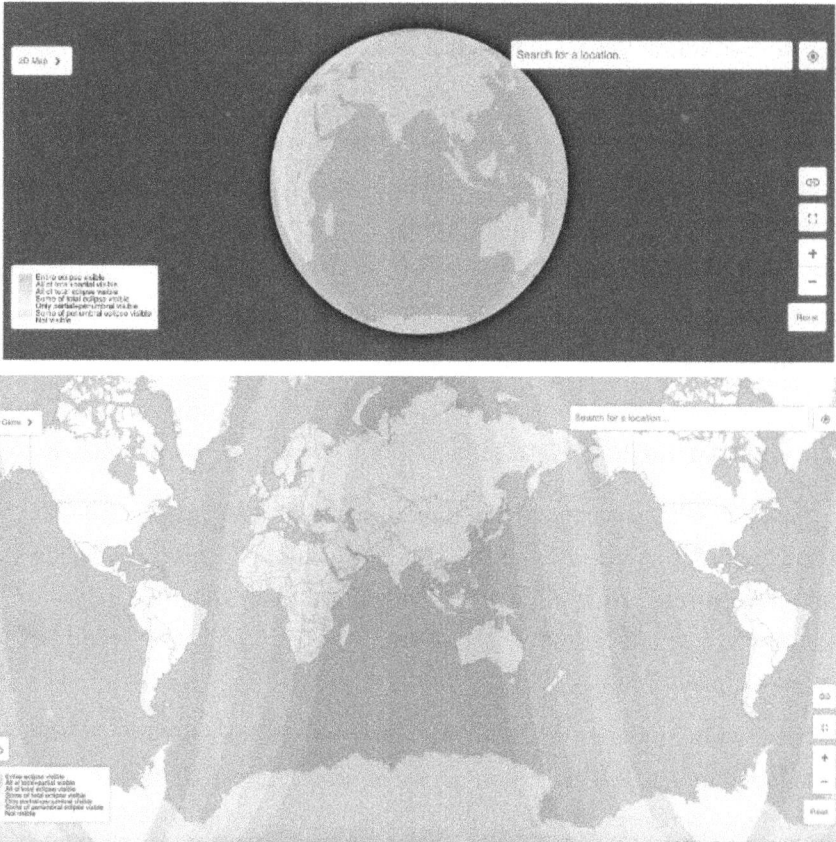

(source: Time and Date)[97]

Rosh Hashanah is the Jewish New Year. It is the anniversary of the creation of Adam and Eve, and a day of judgment and coronation of G-d as king.[98]

---

[97] https://www.timeanddate.com/eclipse/map/2025-september-7

[98] https://www.chabad.org/holidays/default_cdo/year/2025/jewish/holidays-2025.htm

7.6 Joel's Prophecy

In Acts 2:16-20, assumed to be written by Luke, who quotes Joel 2:30-32 and both seem to reflect the signs of Revelation 6, the Sixth Seal which is written by the last living apostle John, inspired by Jesus Christ.

Joel is a prophet and scholars date the book to ~500 B.C. as it refers to the destruction of the 1st temple in Jerusalem (586 B.C.) and exile to Babylon.

Key themes in Joel are summarized briefly as a warning of a "Day of the Lord". A future judgement across all nations and repentance, yet the Lord will turn judgement to blessing through the outpouring of the Spirit. Thus Joel's prophecy of the blood moon is related to the "Day of the Lord" and judgement of the nations.

How rare are the 2025 blood moons?

7.7 2025 Blood Moons Rarity?

In 2025, between the two blood moons, the **entire Earth's major continents** are covered within a six month window. Is this a sign? How rare is this event? How often do two blood moons cover all the nation-states with a dim orange - red blood colored light… as if Jesus shed His blood for the world?

After searching back to 1900, total lunar eclipses are not rare, however, two blood moons that line up in the same year to cover **all major continents** appears to be **very** rare. There is one pair of 1902 blood moons, which seem to come close to covering all continents and another single blood moon in 1945 covers 4 continents, excluding Asia. The two blood moons, in 2025, that cover all major nation-states, appear to be unique at least since 1900.

Chapter 8. Probability of Blood Moons & The Mazzaroth Signs

This is a continuation of the *Prophecy and Probability* study based upon <u>Revelation 6 the Sixth Seal analysis</u> of the astronomical and geological signs that are potentially being unveiled in real-time. My hope is this study of science, statistics, and scripture will build up the perseverance of the saints.

8.1 Blood Moon Buzz

The blood moons have been generating a lot of buzz in bible prophecy circles. Most recently the 2022 Election Day Blood Moon created a massive amount of articles and analysis. Here are just a few links:

- **Hagee, J. (2013). Four Blood Moons: Something is About to Change. Hagee Ministries.Worthy Books; First Edition (October 8, 2013**)

- **Armstrong, S.. (2015). Four Blood Moons. Verse by Verse Ministry.**

- **Meffert, C. and Joiner, J. (2022). Election Day Blood Moon won't happen again until 2394. The Hill.**

But let's look a little closer at these blood moons. Below are the four blood moons noted by J. Hagee and S. Armstrong. The first one is aligned over the Americas. The next three are aligned over oceans: Pacific, Pacific, and Atlantic. God can do the impossible, why miss the continents and only give them a partial blood moon?

Fig 8.1 2014 and 2015 Four Blood Moons

Eclipses in 2014

Apr 14–15   Lunar Eclipse (Total)

Oct 7–8   Lunar Eclipse (Total)

Eclipses in 2015

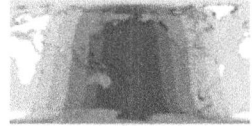

Apr 4   Lunar Eclipse (Total)

Sep 27–28   Lunar Eclipse (Total)

(Source: Time and Date)[99]

The 2022 Election Day Blood Moon on November 7-8th, 2022, nearly missed North America completely. The best place to view the blood moon eclipse was probably from Hawaii.

Nov 7–8   Lunar Eclipse (Total)

Why are the above blood moons so inaccurate, to the point that they are not visible **whole blood moons**? They would have been a partial blood

[99] https://www.timeanddate.com/eclipse/list-total-lunar.html?starty=2010

moon or a pink moon. God's astronomical clock has been pretty accurate so far with:

- **An Earthquake and aftershock in Turkey where the 7 Churches of Revelation were planted.**

- And two Great Solar Eclipses over North America covering 20 Salems and a Cross of Peace in the center.

God's aim has been on-target to a variance of 500 meters (see Salem Rd), and His accuracy is going to continue in 2025 with two blood moons that cover every continent of the world perfectly so the whole world will see the whole moon turn to blood. Hard to believe, but true.

What is the probability of the Earthquake and aftershock, two solar eclipses, **and two total lunar eclipses where the whole moon became like blood**?

> **Answer:** *1/(2.6592e+12).* = one in two trillion six hundred fifty-nine billion two hundred million
>
> Show work below

To review the blood moon analysis:

8.2 A Total Lunar Eclipse

The National Oceanic and Atmospheric Association (NOAA) states, that during a total lunar eclipse, the sequence of eclipses are: penumbral, partial, **total,** partial and back to penumbral.[100]

That Earth's atmosphere scatters blue light, thus only red light remains when the moon is in a perfect total eclipse. A total lunar eclipse casts its red light across continents and/or oceans. Thus a blood moon is visible

---

[100] https://www.weather.gov/fsd/suneclipse#:~:text=For%20an%20eclipse%20to%20occur,year%20instead%20of%20every%20month.

simultaneously across a very large region of the Earth. A total lunar eclipse occurs approximately once every 1.5 years on average.[101]

> Probability of a total lunar eclipse is 1 out of 1.5 = 1/1.5
>
> Probability of 2 independent total lunar eclipses is 1/(1.5 x 1.5) = 1/2.25

But what does it mean that the *whole* moon became like blood?

8.3 Word Study: "whole"

> I looked when He broke the sixth seal, and
> there was a great Earthquake; and
> the sun became black as sackcloth made of hair, and
> the **whole** moon became like **blood;**
> and the stars of the sky fell to the Earth, as a fig tree casts its
> unripe figs when shaken by a great wind.
>
> Revelation 6:12-13, NASB1995

Note the "*whole* moon became like *blood*".

"Whole" in Greek is *holos*:

> **Usage:** all, the whole, entire, complete.[102]

Holos is used in the Bible 110 times. Apostle John may have had a reason in using the literal term *whole* to describe the moon bathed in blood. He did not want future readers to miss out on this key sign. The whole or "entire eclipse is visible" **only** when the eclipse is "perfect" and the shadow casts a red light on the moon. It is not a partial shadow on the moon, but the *whole* moon becomes cast in blood red light which is visible by man on Earth, if they are on a continent aligned under the moon. Let's analyze the word "blood" in Scripture.

---

[101] Ridgeway, B. (2022). Last Chance to See Total Lunar Eclipse Until 2025!. NASA. https://ephesians610.substack.com/publish/post/120206535

[102] https://biblehub.com/text/revelation/6-12.htm

8.4 Word Study: "blood"

"Blood" in Greek is *haima*:

Usage: blood (especially as shed).[103]

Haima is used in the Bible 98 times. In Revelation, Apostle John uses it 19 times. Blood is used to describe:

• Revelation 1:5 <u>NAS:</u> releasing us from our sins *by His blood--*

• Revelation 6:10 <u>NAS:</u> and avenging *our blood* on those who dwell on Earth…

• Revelation 6:12 <u>NAS:</u> the moon became like *blood;*

• Revelation 7:14 <u>NAS:</u> and made them white *in the blood* of the Lamb.

• Revelation 8:8 <u>NAS:</u> and a third of the sea became *blood,*

• and it continues with the <u>blood of the saints, prophets, witnesses…</u> and more.

Literally: The total lunar eclipse is the color of *blood (haima).*

Symbolically: The *blood* may mean the blood of Jesus shed for the whole world or the blood shed by others on Earth or a harbinger ("something that foreshadows a future event : something that gives an anticipatory sign of what is to come"[104])…. only time will tell.

Will the *blood* moons be visible to the *whole* Earth?

Weather permitting it definitely will be in 2025…

8.5 Blood Moons Visible by the Whole World

There are no total lunar eclipses in 2023 or 2024. In 2025 there are two total lunar eclipses where people can see the *whole moon become like blood* from **ALL** major continents and nation states of the world. Let's take a look at this closer. Is this just coincidence or a harbinger?

---

[103] https://biblehub.com/greek/129.htm

[104] https://www.merriam-webster.com/dictionary/harbinger

March 13-14th, 2025: The *whole* moon will become like blood over the Americas. September 7-8th, 2025: The *whole* moon will become like blood over the rest of the world including: Russia, Asia, India, Europe, the Middle East, Australia, and Africa. Though it is not rare to have 2 blood moons in 1 year, it is rare to see two blood moons, in the same year, that cover all major continents and nation states, where the whole moon becoming like blood, is visible in entirety for the whole world. The two blood moons are also separated by 178 days which is ~6 Prophetic Months, where each month is 30 days.

8.6 A Pair of 1902 Blood Moons in the Mazzaroth

The last time two blood moons were visible to ALL continents was in **1902**. For reference there are two **1902** eclipses. The first is April 22-23, 1902 over Asia, India, Australia, Middle East, Europe, and Africa.[105] The second blood moon is October 16-17, 1902 over the Americas.[106] The two blood moons are also separated by 178 days which is ~6 Prophetic Months of 30 days each month. Coincidentally **1902** is also a historical marker in Jewish history.

Russian Pograms were large-scale anti-Jewish riots that erupted in 1902. This led to many years of pograms which instilled hate, persecution, and death. The killing continued through WWI and WWII.[107] As events on Earth unfolded leading up to World Wars, the following Heavenly signs are highlighted by the blood moons.

This section has been augmented to further analyze the two lunar eclipses of 1902. Similar to the solar eclipses of 2017, 2023, and 2024, let's look up at the Mazzaroth signs which are highlighted by the eclipses.

The April 22nd, 1902 blood moon appears less than 10 degrees below the star Spica, the seed or branch. This is a repeating theme in the Heavens which brings us to Genesis 3:15, the "Seed of the Woman".

---

[105] https://www.timeanddate.com/eclipse/map/1902-april-22

[106] https://www.timeanddate.com/eclipse/globe/1902-october-17

[107] https://www.history.com/topics/european-history/pogroms

Fig 8.6.1 April 22, 1902 - Total Lunar Eclipse - Virgo

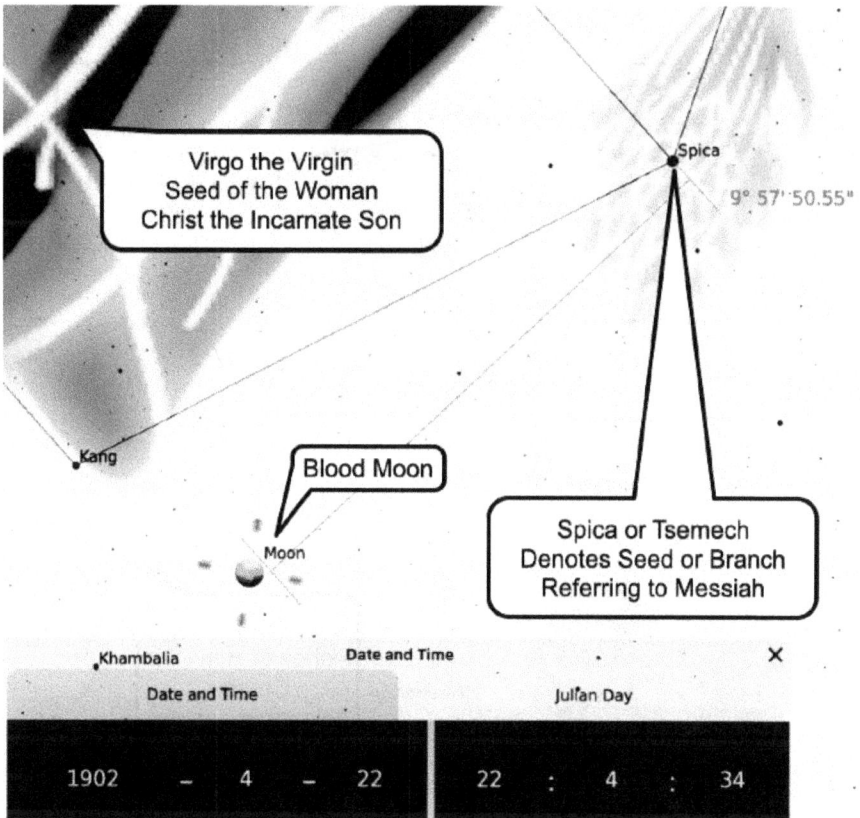

The blood shed on the Cross washes away the sins of the world. The April 22nd, 1902 blood moon casts blood red over half the Earth.

The October 16th, 1902 blood moon is located between the two fish in Pisces as they play tug-o-war with Cetus, casting red over the Americas. Pisces, representing Christians, has two stars Okda, denotes the united, and Alsamaca denotes the upheld. Cetus, the Beast of the Sea, in 1902 is likely the British Imperial Empire.

Fig 8.6.2 October 16, 1902 - Total Lunar Eclipse - Pisces

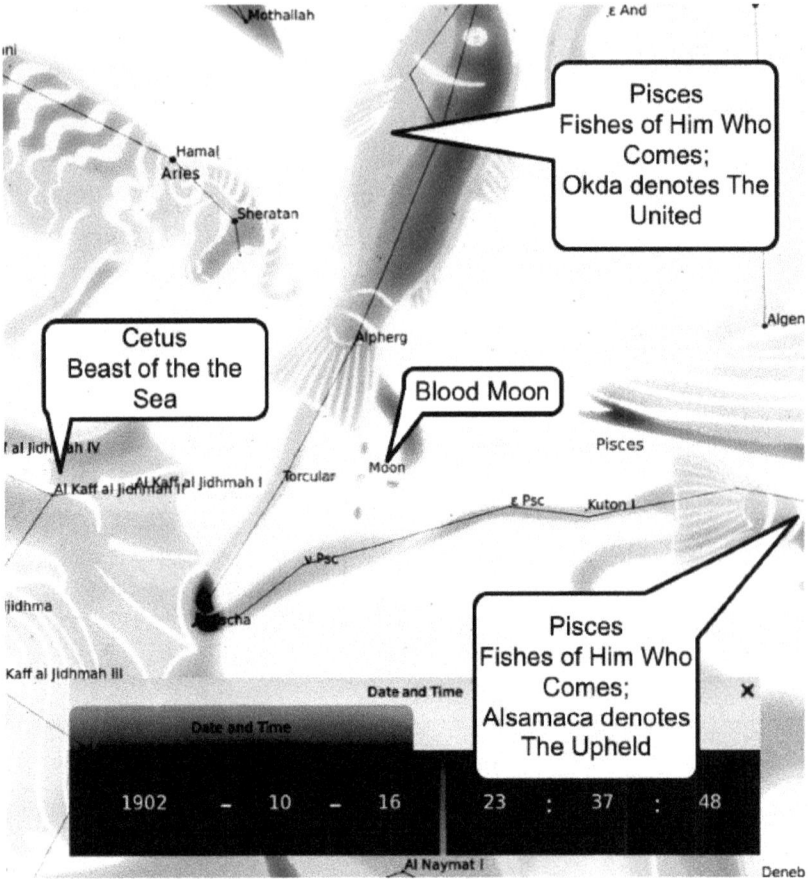

Imperialism set the stage for World War I (WWI).[108] Expansion of empires created tensions between nations which resulted in conflict as a key cause of WWI. At the end of WWI, in 1920, the League of Nations was formed. In 1945, the United Nations (UN) was formed to replace the League of Nations. Seventy-Five years later, the WHO, a subsidiary, of the UN, declared the Global Plandemic on March 11th, 2020. Could the 1902 blood moons have ushered in the beginning of what we see today as a multi-national global government. Also notice the 1902 blood moon Total

---

[108] https://www.history.com/articles/imperialism-causes-world-war-i

Lunar Eclipse parallels the 2024 Total Solar Eclipse. See Fig 6.4.4 for the April 8th, 2024: Total Solar Eclipse between Cetus and Pisces which falls directly on the rope which is very similar to the October 16th, 1902 blood moon which falls between the "V" of the ropes between the two fish and Cetus.

8.7 The 2025 Blood Moon Near Virgo

This section has been added to further analyze the two lunar eclipses of 2025. Let's review the Mazzaroth signs which are highlighted by the eclipses.

Fig 8.7.1 March 14th, 2025 Total Lunar Eclipse - Virgo

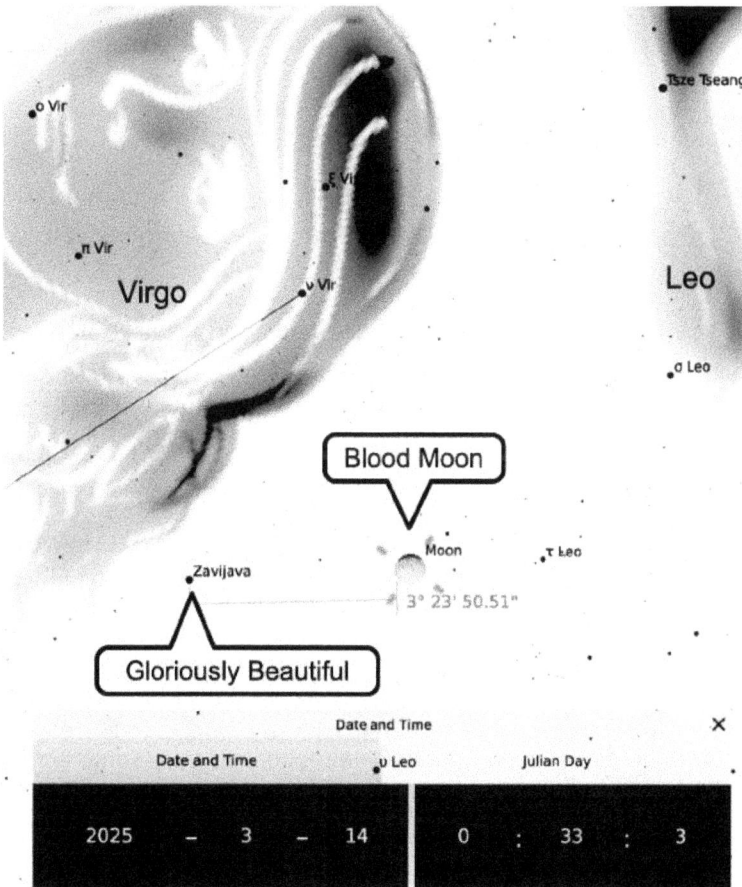

The first total lunar eclipse on March 13-14th, 2025 is positioned in the night sky at the head of the virgin near the star *Zavijava*, which denotes *gloriously beautiful*. The star name describes the beautiful glorious birth of Jesus Christ.

> In that day the **branch** of the LORD shall be **beautiful and glorious**, and the fruit of the land shall be the pride and honor of the survivors of Israel. Isaiah 4:2, ESV[109] [emphasis added]

The other stars in the virgin include *Spica* which denotes the seed or branch. Both stars *Spica* and *Zavijava* can be correlated to **branch**. What else can we learn from this Sign in Heaven about the branch?

> The biblical concept of the "Branch" is a rich messianic metaphor with profound theological significance. The Old Testament includes six central passages where "Branch" refers to the coming Messiah.[110]

As John the Baptist states early in the ministry of Jesus,

> The next day he [John the Baptist] saw Jesus coming toward him, and said, "Behold, the Lamb of God, who takes away the sin of the world! John 1:29, ESV[111]

John the Baptist was prophesying the future sacrifice of Jesus, the Messiah, as the Passover Lamb on April 3rd, 33 AD. Jesus was crucified on the cross and His blood washes away the sins of all who believe in Him. On the night that Jesus died on the cross, there was also a blood moon. This is known through ancient historical documents recorded by Pilate and Cyril of Alexandria.[112] The blood moon of April 3rd, 33 AD is similarly positioned at the foot of the virgin. On that night there is a partial lunar

---

[109] The Holy Bible: English Standard Version (Is 4:2). (2016). Crossway Bibles.

[110] Neil Wilson and Nancy Ryken Taylor, in The A to Z Guide to Bible Signs and Symbols: Understanding Their Meaning and Significance (Grand Rapids, MI: Baker Books, 2015), 40.

[111] The Holy Bible: English Standard Version (Jn 1:29). (2016). Crossway Bibles.

[112] https://ephesians610.substack.com/p/communion-crucifixion-and-resurrection#footnote-13-179525473

eclipse and a Paschal moon. The word Paschal denotes Passover, that is a blood red.

Fig 8.7.2 April 3rd, 33 AD Partial Lunar Eclipse - Virgo

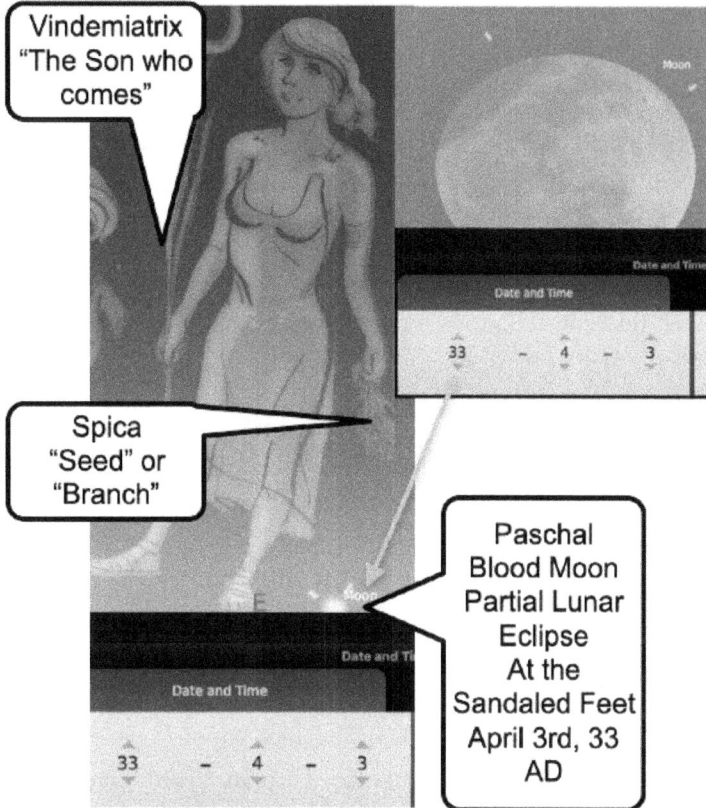

The Paschal moon the night of the crucifixion of Jesus Christ is also at the foot of the virgin. This seems to highlight Genesis 3:15.

> I will put enmity between you and the woman, and between your offspring and her offspring; **he** shall **bruise** your head, and you shall **bruise** his heel." Genesis 3:15, ESV [emph. add.]

Who is "he"? Paul writes,

The **God of peace will soon crush Satan under your feet**.
The grace of our Lord Jesus Christ be with you. Romans
16:20, ESV[11] [emphasis added]

She carries the star *Spica*, the seed or branch, referring to Jesus, Son of God. Jesus shall **bruise and soon crush** Satan's head, and Satan shall **bruise** the Seed of the Woman's heel.

At this point, Satan believes He has won the battle. He has taken a "bite" out of the heel through the Crucifixion of Jesus on the cross. However, just wait… it's all part of God's plan.

The blood moon is also positioned at the foot of the Lion. Both the woman and lion constellations repeat through history from Creation, Noah's Flood, the Birth of Jesus, the Crucifixion, and the Revelation 12 Sign (Reference *The Covenant Signs*).[113] The Lion correlates to the Lion of Judah and its primary star *Regulus*, denoting "little king".

In the right hand of the woman is another branch. In this branch is a star named *Vindemiatrix* which denotes "the Son who comes". Both *Spica* and *Vindemiatrix* therefore can be correlated to the Messiah.

8.8 The 2025 Blood Moon Near Aquarius

The second 2025 Total Lunar Eclipse Blood Moon is positioned near the water pouring from the jug of Aquarius. The star *Hydor*, denotes, water which is within 4 degrees of the moon.

Aquarius denotes Christ the Living water in the Mazzaroth.[114] Apostle John records the story of Jesus and the Samaritan woman at the well,

> [14] but whoever drinks of the water that I will give him will never be thirsty again. The water that I will give him will

---

[113] Law, E. (2024). The Covenant Signs - An Investigation of the Astronomical Signs in God's Covenants & The Star of Bethlehem

[114] https://mazzarothgospel.blogspot.com/

become in him a spring of water welling up to eternal life. John 4:14, ESV[115]

Fig 8.8.1 September 7th, 2025 AD Partial Lunar Eclipse - Virgo

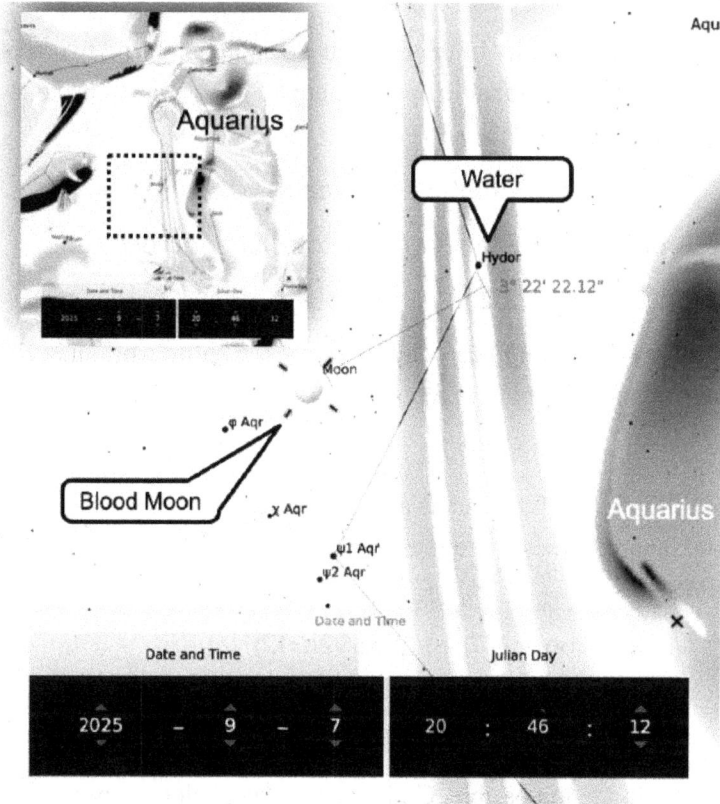

In the Book of Revelation, we are again reminded of the Water of Life,

> Then the angel showed me the river of the **water of life**, bright as crystal, flowing from the throne of God and of the Lamb. Revelation 22:1, ESV[116]

> The Spirit and the Bride say, "Come." And let the one who hears say, "Come." And let the one who is thirsty come; let

---

[115] The Holy Bible: English Standard Version (Jn 4:14). (2016). Crossway Bibles.

[116] The Holy Bible: English Standard Version (Re 22:1). (2016). Crossway Bibles.

the one who desires take the **water of life** without price. Revelation 22:17, ESV[117]

8.9 Probability and Further Study

What is the probability of the Earthquake and aftershock, two solar eclipses, and two total lunar eclipses where the whole moon became like blood for all the nations to see?

Answer: 2025 - 1902 = 123 years

Probability of 2 independent total lunar eclipses is

1/(1.5 x 1.5) = 1/2.25

Probability of 2 total lunar eclipses where the entire world has visibility to the whole moon turning to blood:

1/(123 x 2.25) = 1/277

Probability of the Earthquake and aftershock, two solar eclipses, and two total lunar eclipses where the whole moon became like blood for all the nations to see:

1/(9.6 Billion x 277) = 1/(2.6592e+12)

= one in two trillion six hundred fifty-nine billion two hundred million

God can do the impossible. God's astronomical clock is perfect. Here are some study questions with related bible verses from Apostle John where he talks about *the whole (holos) world.*

2 and He Himself is the propitiation for our sins; and not for ours only, but also for *those of* the **whole world**. 1 John 2:2, NASB1995

19 We know that we are of God, and that the **whole world** lies in *the power of* the evil one. 1 John 5:19, NASB1995

---

[117] The Holy Bible: English Standard Version (Re 22:17). (2016). Crossway Bibles.

10 Because you have kept the word of My perseverance, I also will keep you from the hour of testing, that hour which is about to come upon the **whole world**, to test those who dwell on the Earth. Revelation 3:10, NASB1995

The Day of the Lord

30 "I will display wonders in the sky and on the Earth, Blood, fire and columns of smoke. **31** "The sun will be turned into darkness and the moon into blood before the great and awesome day of the Lord comes. Joel 2:30-31, NASB1995

Questions:

• Is there a supernatural literal meaning behind the whole (*holos*) moon turned to blood for the whole (*holos*) world?

• Is there a supernatural parallel in these signs to remind us that Jesus died and shed His blood for the *whole* world?

• Does the *whole world* lie in the power of the evil one? (See 1 John 5:19)

• Is the hour about to come upon the *whole world*, to test those who dwell on the Earth? (See Revelation 3:10). Has that hour already begun?

Continue to persevere and look up.

Chapter 9. Are Meteor Showers and/or Comets a Sign?

This is a continuation of the Revelation Sixth Seal analysis where we have analyzed

1. **two Earthquakes**,

2. **three solar eclipses**, and

3. **two blood moons**,

4. next on the list, two pairs of "meteor showers":

    1. 2018 and 2025

    2. 1933 and 1946.

    and the **stars of the sky fell to the Earth**,
    as a fig tree casts its unripe figs when shaken by a great
    wind. Revelation 6:13, NASB1995

This article will look at:

• What are meteor showers? What "shakes" meteors and causes them to fall as if by a "great wind"?

• Why are the October Draconid meteor showers special and what causes them? A comet?

• Can we forecast meteor showers that are more intense than others? Can comets be considered a sign?

Several meteor showers have been analyzed, but specifically there seems to be a very interesting pattern with the Draconid meteor showers from the Draco constellation. The Draconid meteor shower is visible from Jerusalem in the northwestern horizon early October each year.

The Draconids are a short-lived meteor shower, and its intensity varies from year to year (i.e.: ~5 to 12000 meteors per hour). Below is a screenshot from Stellarium showing October 9th, 2025 from East Jerusalem. The Draconids are highlighted in blue and radiate from Draco's eye. Notice in 2025 the meteor shower lasts from October 5th to 10th and its maximum is October 8th.

9.1 The Mazzaroth and Draco

In the ancient Mazzaroth (Hebrew for constellation), Draco is the dragon and associated with other serpents and scorpion in the stars.

The constellation Draco, the Great Serpent, was at one time ruler of the night, being formerly at the very centre of the Heavens and so large that it was called the Great Dragon.[118]

The dragon is primarily described in Revelation 12 as the fiery red dragon, Satan, the serpent of old. And the great dragon was thrown down, the serpent of old who is called the devil and Satan, who deceives the whole world; he was thrown down to the Earth, and his angels were thrown down with him. (Revelation 12:9-10)

Draco (Greek) means "troddon on"[119] and even in the screenshot, above, the dragon's head faces down as if "thrown down to Earth". The star names in Draco also reflect the ancient meaning of the dragon:

- Thuban = "the subtle or large snake"

- Ethanin = "the long serpent", "great serpent", or "dragon"

- Rastaban (Heb) = "the head of the subtle serpent or dragon"

- Al Waid (Arabic) = "who is to be destroyed"[120,121]

---

[118] https://www.sacred-texts.com/wmn/wb/wb73.htm

[119] https://biblenumbers.files.wordpress.com/2017/06/ad-era-27-draco-1301-to-1350.pdf

[120] https://www.bereaninsights.org/nugget/the-message-in-the-stars-sagittarius/

[121] https://mazzarothgospel.blogspot.com/

The dragon has non-retractable claws like a hyena as indicated in the star names. The dragon names also seem to indicate a goat in its claw as in a fresh kill. As in Revelation 12, the dragon is a type of serpent of old, Satan. The fiery red dragon is out to devour the woman and those that follow the commands of Jesus Christ (Revelation 12).

Let's move from the supernatural to the science behind this Heavenly phenomenon.

Fig 9.1.1 Draco and Draconids October 9th, 2025

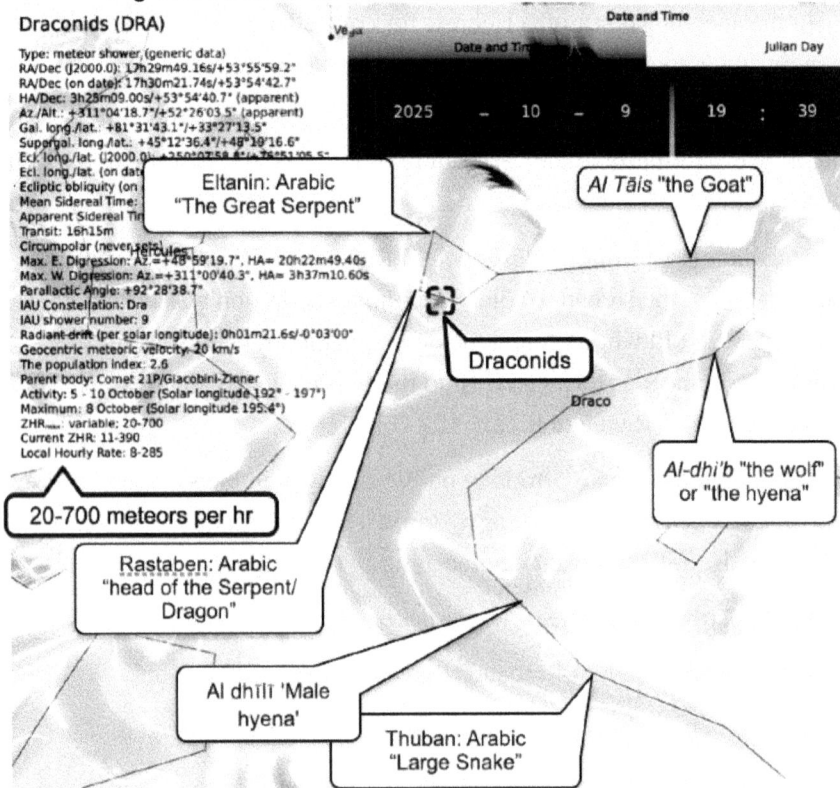

Draconids (DRA)

Type: meteor shower (generic data)
RA/Dec (J2000.0): 17h29m49.16s/+53°55'59.2"
RA/Dec (on date): 17h30m21.74s/+53°54'42.7"
HA/Dec: 3h25m09.00s/+53°54'40.7" (apparent)
Az./Alt.: +311°04'18.7"/+52°26'03.5" (apparent)
Gal. long./lat.: +81°31'43.1"/+33°27'13.5"
Supergal. long./lat.: +45°12'36.4"/+48°19'16.6"
Ecl. long./lat. (J2000.0):
Ecl. long./lat. (on date)
Ecliptic obliquity (on
Mean Sidereal Time:
Apparent Sidereal Ti
Transit: 16h15m
Circumpolar (never sets)
Max. E. Digression: Az.=+48°59'19.7", HA= 20h22m49.40s
Max. W. Digression: Az.=+311°00'40.3", HA= 3h37m10.60s
Parallactic Angle: +92°28'38.7"
IAU Constellation: Dra
IAU shower number: 9
Radiant drift (per solar longitude): 0h01m21.6s/-0°03'00"
Geocentric meteoric velocity: 20 km/s
The population index: 2.6
Parent body: Comet 21P/Giacobini-Zinner
Activity: 5 - 10 October (Solar longitude 192° - 197°)
Maximum: 8 October (Solar longitude 195.4°)
ZHR: variable: 20-700
Current ZHR: 11-390
Local Hourly Rate: 8-285

Date and Time

		Date and Time				Julian Day
2025	–	10	–	9	19 :	39

Eltanin: Arabic "The Great Serpent"

Al Tāis "the Goat"

Draconids

Draco

Al-dhi'b "the wolf" or "the hyena"

20-700 meteors per hr

Rastaben: Arabic "head of the Serpent/ Dragon"

Al dhīlī 'Male hyena'

Thuban: Arabic "Large Snake"

(source: Stellarium)

9.2 What are Meteor Showers?

Here are some astronomical facts:

- Meteors occur when cosmic debris, comet particles, broken asteroids, and particles hit the Earth's atmosphere and create a fiery streak in the sky.

- Comets fly in from the great expanse beyond the firmament and pass close to our sun and the Earth. The comet tail leaves a trail of cosmic dust particles that can lead to meteors.

- Meteor showers can be forecasted much like the weather.[122]

- Meteor showers are named after the constellations that they radiate from. For example, the Draconids originate from the constellation Draco the dragon. Leonids originate from Leo the lion. Perseids appear from Perseus.

- From Earth, each meteor shower radiates from a point in the sky called the radiant.

- Meteors enter the Earth's atmosphere and are typically the size of a sand grain. Some meteors are the size of peas or marbles.[123]

In this article, A Meteor Wind Over Tunisia. **Does the Earth ever pass through a wind of meteors?** *Yes*, and they are frequently visible as meteor showers where it can appear as a **meteor wind**.[124]

---

[122] https://solarsystem.nasa.gov/asteroids-comets-and-meteors/meteors-and-meteorites/lyrids/in-depth/

[123] https://sites.wustl.edu/meteoritesite/items/meteors/#:~:text=Space.com%3A%20%E2%80%9CPerseid%20meteoroids,big%20as%20peas%20or%20marbles.

[124] https://science.nasa.gov/meteor-wind-over-tunisia

9.3 Forecasting Meteor Showers

Every year there are multiple meteor showers radiating from various constellations. Figure 9.3.1 plots the intensity of meteor showers over a year.

On October 7th, 2022, "The 2023 meteor shower activity forecast for low Earth orbit"[125], is posted by the NASA Meteoroid Environment Office. The Y-axis is the Zenithal Hourly Rate (ZHR), and the X-axis are the months

Fig 9.3.1 Meteor Showers Graph by ZHR for 2023

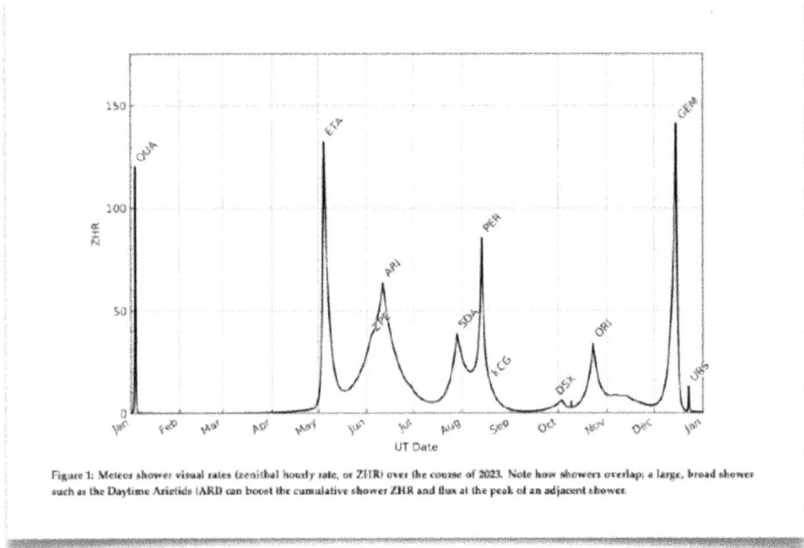

Figure 1: Meteor shower visual rates (zenithal hourly rate, or ZHR) over the course of 2023. Note how showers overlap; a large, broad shower such as the Daytime Arietids (ARD) can boost the cumulative shower ZHR and flux at the peak of an adjacent shower.

(Source: **NASA NTRS**)[126]

ZHR is "the number of meteors a single observer would see in an hour of peak activity if it was at the zenith."[127]

---

[125] Moorhead, A, Moser, D, & Cooke, B. (2023). The 2023 meteor shower activity forecast for low Earth orbit. NASA NTRS. **https://ntrs.nasa.gov/citations/20230001681**

[126] Ibid.

[127] https://en.wikipedia.org/wiki/Zenithal_hourly_rate

The October Draconids (DRA) have a max **ZHR of 3** which is not very high compared to the Geminids (GEM) with a max ZHR of 140. In the graph above DRA shows up as a tiny spike on October 9th, 2023.

Fig 9.3.2 Meteor Showers Table by ZHR for 2023

shower name	ID	max time (UT)	max ZHR
Quadrantids	QUA	2023-01-04 00:25	120
eta Aquariids	ETA	2023-05-04 12:31	129
Daytime zeta Perseids	ZPE	2023-06-03 12:08	20
Daytime Arietids	ARI	2023-06-11 04:46	50
Southern mu Sagittariids	SSG	2023-06-20 09:19	2
beta Taurids	BTA	2023-06-28 23:36	2
Southern delta Aquariids	SDA	2023-07-28 13:49	30
alpha Capricornids	CAP	2023-07-29 03:38	4
Perseids	PER	2023-08-13 08:50	80
kappa Cygnids	KCG	2023-08-18 12:27	5
Daytime Sextantids	DSX	2023-10-03 05:45	5
October Draconids	DRA	2023-10-09 07:48	3
Orionids	ORI	2023-10-23 04:25	30
Southern Taurids	STA	2023-11-06 00:32	5
Northern Taurids	NTA	2023-11-12 23:47	5
Geminids	GEM	2023-12-14 19:59	140
Ursids	URS	2023-12-22 16:23	12

Table 3: Meteor showers in 2023. Column 2 provides the 3-letter code for each shower, Column 3 lists the date and time of maximum activity, and Column 4 provides the shower's ZHR at the time of maximum activity.

(Source: NASA NTRS)[128]

Some of the meteor showers above are not visible from Jerusalem during specific times of the year due to the horizon or due to a full moon. Also the Geminids and Aquarrids seem to have a very stable ZHR with very little variation year over year. The October Draconids are not as consistent and vary considerably. Let's look at the astronomical reasons for this variation.

The 2025 meteor showers are shown in Figure 9.3.3.

---

[128] Moorhead, A, Moser, D, & Cooke, B. (2023). The 2023 meteor shower activity forecast for low Earth orbit. NASA NTRS. https://ntrs.nasa.gov/citations/20230001681

Fig 9.3.3 Meteor Showers Graph by ZHR for 2025

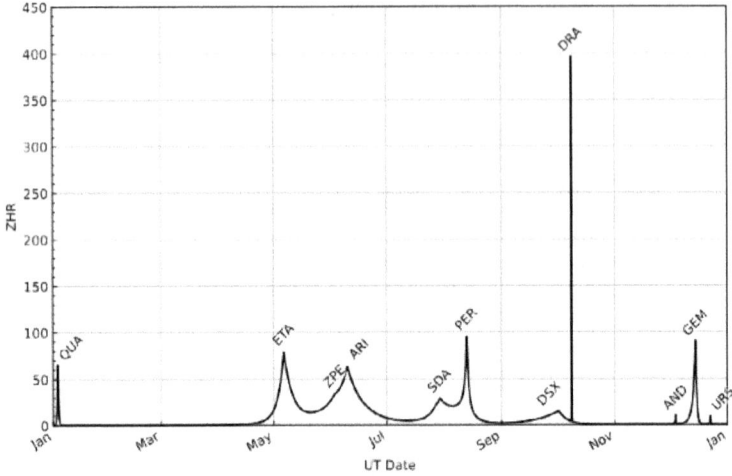

Figure 1: Meteor shower visual rates (zenithal hourly rate, or ZHR) over the course of 2025. Note how showers overlap; a large, broad shower such as the Daytime Arietids (ARI) can boost the cumulative shower ZHR and flux at the peak of an adjacent shower such as the Daytime zeta Perseids (ZPE).

Notice the difference between 2023 and 2025. The DRA or Draconids in 2025 reached nearly 400 ZHR or 400 meteors in a single hour which is significantly higher than 2023, which was 3 ZHR.

Fig 9.3.4 Meteor Showers Table by ZHR for 2025

shower name	ID	date of maximum (UT)	max ZHR
Quadrantids	QUA	2025-01-03 12:27	65
eta Aquariids	ETA	2025-05-06 10:16	75
Daytime zeta Perseids	ZPE	2025-06-03 00:34	20
Daytime Arietids	ARI	2025-06-09 19:49	49
Southern mu Sagittariids	SSG	2025-06-19 21:50	2
Southern delta Aquariids	SDA	2025-07-29 18:26	20
alpha Capricornids	CAP	2025-07-30 22:16	3
Perseids	PER	2025-08-13 08:01	92
Daytime Sextantids	DSX	2025-10-01 17:25	15
October Draconids	DRA	2025-10-08 15:46	394
Andromedids	AND	2025-12-03 09:16	10
Geminids	GEM	2025-12-14 06:55	90
Ursids	URS	2025-12-22 09:44	9

Table 3: Meteor showers in 2025. Column 2 provides the 3-letter code for each shower, column 3 lists the date and time of maximum activity, and column 4 provides the shower's ZHR at the time of maximum activity.

9.4 What causes the Draconids?

The Draconids, radiating from the constellation Draco, are caused by particles released from comet 21P/Giacobini-Zinner, which is categorized as a Jupiter-family comet, comparable in size to Mount Everest (~2km diameter). It is classified as a Near Earth Asteroid (NEA) and not a potential hazard to Earth. 21P comet completes its cycle every 2,390 days (6.54 years). Each time it comes near the Earth, it will spray particles which then form the Draconids. Giacobini-Zinner reached perihelion (closest approach to the Sun) in the year 2012, 2018, and 2025.

> The Draconids radiate out of the northern constellation of Draco the dragon. Most years the shower is weak, and many times very few meteors are seen. However, there are also Draconid meteor storms (sometimes called Giacobinid meteors) on record. A meteor storm is observed when one thousand or more meteors are seen per hour at the location of the observer. During its peak in 1933, **500 Draconid meteors were seen per minute in Europe**. 1946 was also a good year for the Draconids, where **50 -100 were seen per minute in the U.S.**[129]

Read that again: "500 per minute", "50-100 per minute"... how could that be?

The 1933 and 1946 outbursts are recorded in history as a significant meteor shower and both can verified in Stellarium. In the following section the 1933 and 1946 meteor storm outbursts will be verified in Stellarium. Furthermore the path of the comet will also be traced through the Mazzaroth for both 1933 and 1946 to investigate the signs.

---

[129] https://solarsystem.nasa.gov/asteroids-comets-and-meteors/comets/21p-giacobini-zinner/in-depth/

9.5 1933 and 1946 Meteor Storms

Fig 9.5.1 Draconids 1933 - 10,000 ZHR

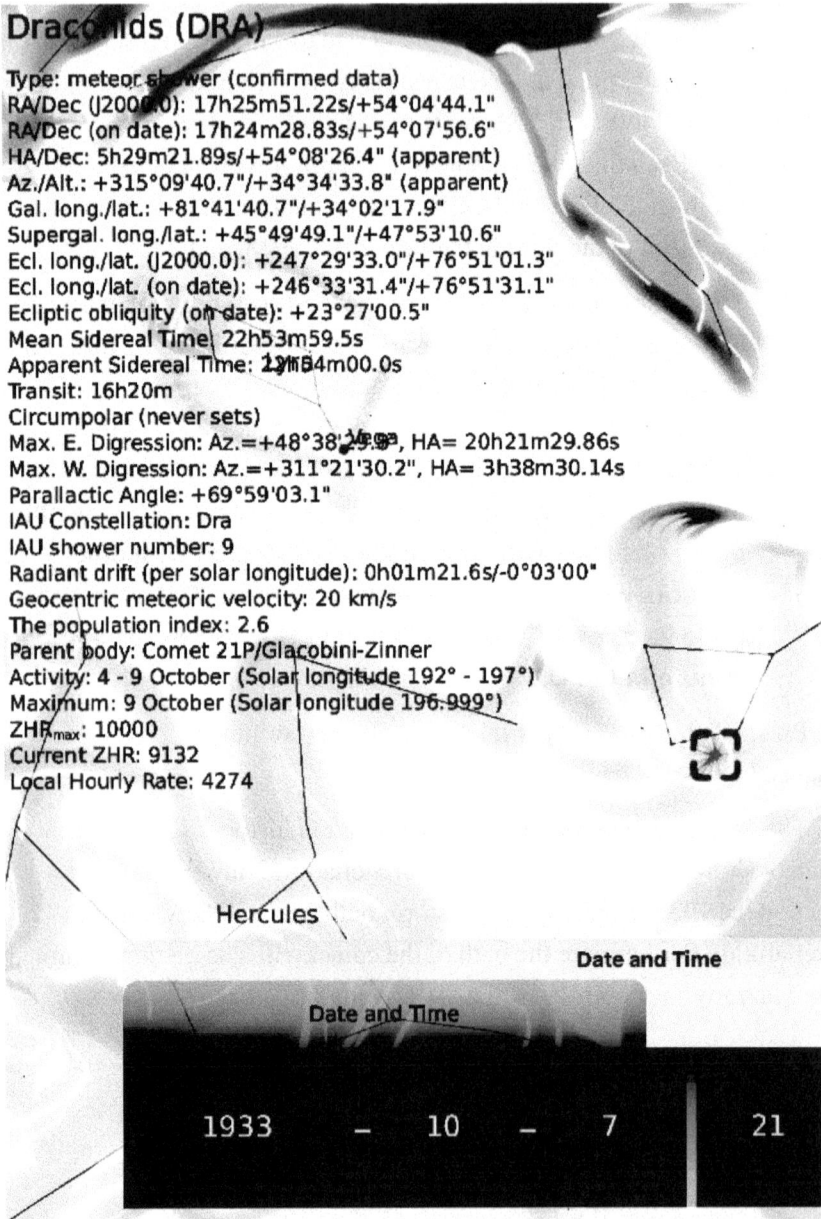

Draconids (DRA)

Type: meteor shower (confirmed data)
RA/Dec (J2000.0): 17h25m51.22s/+54°04'44.1"
RA/Dec (on date): 17h24m28.83s/+54°07'56.6"
HA/Dec: 5h29m21.89s/+54°08'26.4" (apparent)
Az./Alt.: +315°09'40.7"/+34°34'33.8" (apparent)
Gal. long./lat.: +81°41'40.7"/+34°02'17.9"
Supergal. long./lat.: +45°49'49.1"/+47°53'10.6"
Ecl. long./lat. (J2000.0): +247°29'33.0"/+76°51'01.3"
Ecl. long./lat. (on date): +246°33'31.4"/+76°51'31.1"
Ecliptic obliquity (on date): +23°27'00.5"
Mean Sidereal Time: 22h53m59.5s
Apparent Sidereal Time: 22h54m00.0s
Transit: 16h20m
Circumpolar (never sets)
Max. E. Digression: Az.=+48°38'45.9", HA= 20h21m29.86s
Max. W. Digression: Az.=+311°21'30.2", HA= 3h38m30.14s
Parallactic Angle: +69°59'03.1"
IAU Constellation: Dra
IAU shower number: 9
Radiant drift (per solar longitude): 0h01m21.6s/-0°03'00"
Geocentric meteoric velocity: 20 km/s
The population index: 2.6
Parent body: Comet 21P/Giacobini-Zinner
Activity: 4 - 9 October (Solar longitude 192° - 197°)
Maximum: 9 October (Solar longitude 196.999°)
ZHR$_{max}$: 10000
Current ZHR: 9132
Local Hourly Rate: 4274

Hercules

Date and Time

Date and Time

1933 — 10 — 7 21

(Source: Stellarium shows Draconids at 10,000 ZHR in 1933)

Fig. 9.5.2 Draconids 1946 - 12,000 ZHR

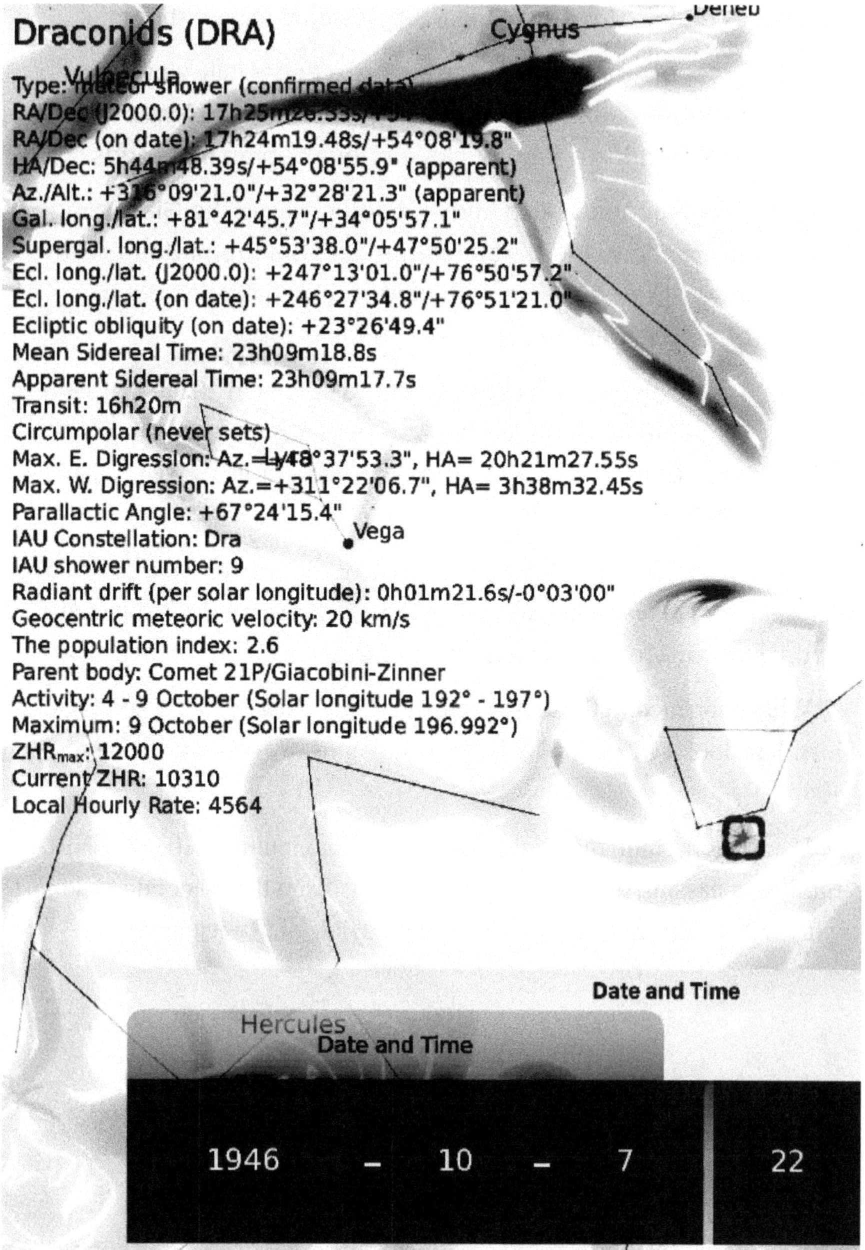

Draconids (DRA)

Type: meteor shower (confirmed data)
RA/Dec (J2000.0): 17h25m26.33s/+54...
RA/Dec (on date): 17h24m19.48s/+54°08'19.8"
HA/Dec: 5h44m48.39s/+54°08'55.9" (apparent)
Az./Alt.: +316°09'21.0"/+32°28'21.3" (apparent)
Gal. long./lat.: +81°42'45.7"/+34°05'57.1"
Supergal. long./lat.: +45°53'38.0"/+47°50'25.2"
Ecl. long./lat. (J2000.0): +247°13'01.0"/+76°50'57.2"
Ecl. long./lat. (on date): +246°27'34.8"/+76°51'21.0"
Ecliptic obliquity (on date): +23°26'49.4"
Mean Sidereal Time: 23h09m18.8s
Apparent Sidereal Time: 23h09m17.7s
Transit: 16h20m
Circumpolar (never sets)
Max. E. Digression: Az.=Ly48°37'53.3", HA= 20h21m27.55s
Max. W. Digression: Az.=+311°22'06.7", HA= 3h38m32.45s
Parallactic Angle: +67°24'15.4"
IAU Constellation: Dra
IAU shower number: 9
Radiant drift (per solar longitude): 0h01m21.6s/-0°03'00"
Geocentric meteoric velocity: 20 km/s
The population index: 2.6
Parent body: Comet 21P/Giacobini-Zinner
Activity: 4 - 9 October (Solar longitude 192° - 197°)
Maximum: 9 October (Solar longitude 196.992°)
ZHR$_{max}$: 12000
Current ZHR: 10310
Local Hourly Rate: 4564

(Source: Stellarium shows Draconids at 12,000 ZHR in 1946)

Pete Lawrence, astronomer and astrophotographer, publishes the following article, "How to see the 2021 Draconid meteor shower",

> Draconid meteor shower trails are especially slow, the meteoroids entering Earth's atmosphere at 21km/s — less than one-third the speed of November's Leonid meteorids.
>
> The Draconids (also known unofficially as the Giacobinids, in reference to the parent **comet 21P/Giacobini-Zinner**) have a low ZHR peak value, but increased activity has been observed over the past few years.
>
> The shower put on spectacular displays in **1933 and 1946,** with ZHR rates measured at thousands of meteors per hour. Enhanced rates were also seen in 1998, 2005, 2011 and 2012.[130]

The year 1933 and 1946 had thousands of meteors per hour, 50 to 500 per minute. This is technically not just a meteor shower, it's a meteor storm, hurricane, or atmospheric river of meteors.

What happened in those two years that impacted the Jews and Israel? First let's look at **1933?** The Holocaust begins in 1933 and ends in 1945.[131]

Using Stellarium, the Draconids reach a maximum of 10,000 ZHR. The Earth was passing through the trail of debris from the comet that had just whipped passed, causing the incredible 10,000 ZHR meteor storm.

---

[130] https://www.skyatnightmagazine.com/advice/draconid-meteor-shower/

[131] https://www.museumoftolerance.com/education/teacher-resources/holocaust-resources/timeline-of-the-holocaust.html

The Nuremberg Tribunals were held in Germany from 1945 to 1946. In the Middle East: Israel's War of Independence was one of the bloodiest of Israel's wars where 6,373 were killed in action.[132] Israel was recognized as a nation on May 14th, 1948.

9.6 The 1933 and 1946 Comet Paths

We're looking back at these unique meteor showers caused by a periodic comet 21P to see if we can gain some knowledge from the Mazzaroth. In

---

[132] https://embassies.gov.il/MFA/AboutIsrael/history/Pages/
Israels%20War%20of%20Independence%20-%201947%20-%201949.aspx

both Fig. 9.8.1 and 9.8.2, the Draconids are shown coming from the eye of Draco the dragon (See top-left of screenshot)

Fig. 9.6.1 Comet 21P Path in 1933

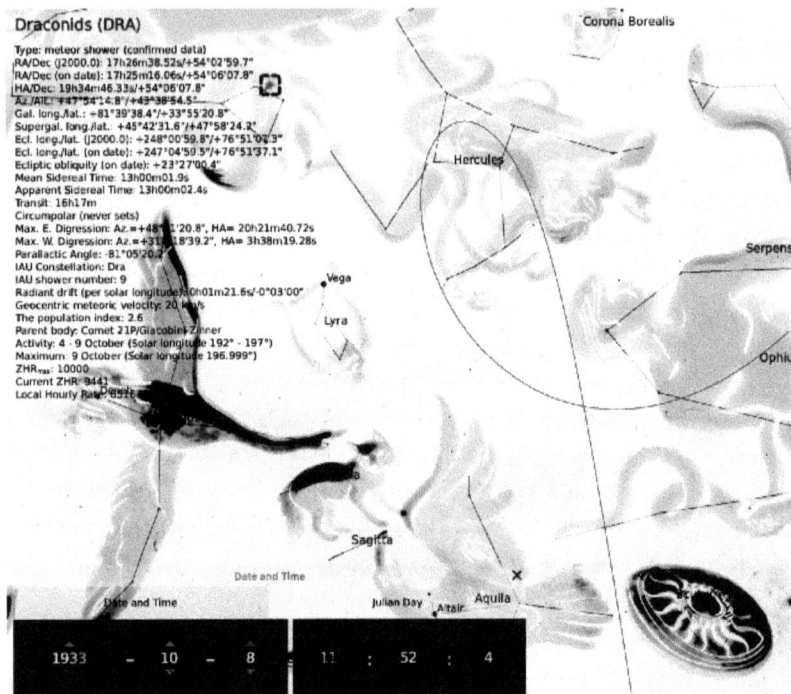

(Source: Stellarium)

In 1933, 21P/Giacobini-Zinner starts in the constellation of Ophiucus, the serpent holder. Ophiucus is also known as Asclepius, the god of medicine. The periodic comet then makes a loop around Hercules, the man wrestling with a three headed Hydra. Hercules as you can see in Figure 9.8.1 has his foot upon Draco the dragon's head. Given this celestial storyboard, Hercules seems to be a Christ-like figure battling the serpent of old, the Dragon (Genesis 3:15, Revelation 12). Then the comet heads down to the lower right past Aquila, the eagle in flight, associated with the First Living Creature and the Shield of Faith, Scutum, as described in *The Signs of the Four Horsemen* (Revelation 6, Ephesians 6).

In 1946, the periodic comet makes a similar loop from Ophiucus around Hercules before heading down between Aquila and Scutum. In both years the comet draws a distinct story highlighting spiritual war between the serpent of old, the dragon, Satan, and those that follow the commands of Jesus Christ.

Fig. 9.6.2 Comet 21P Path in 1946

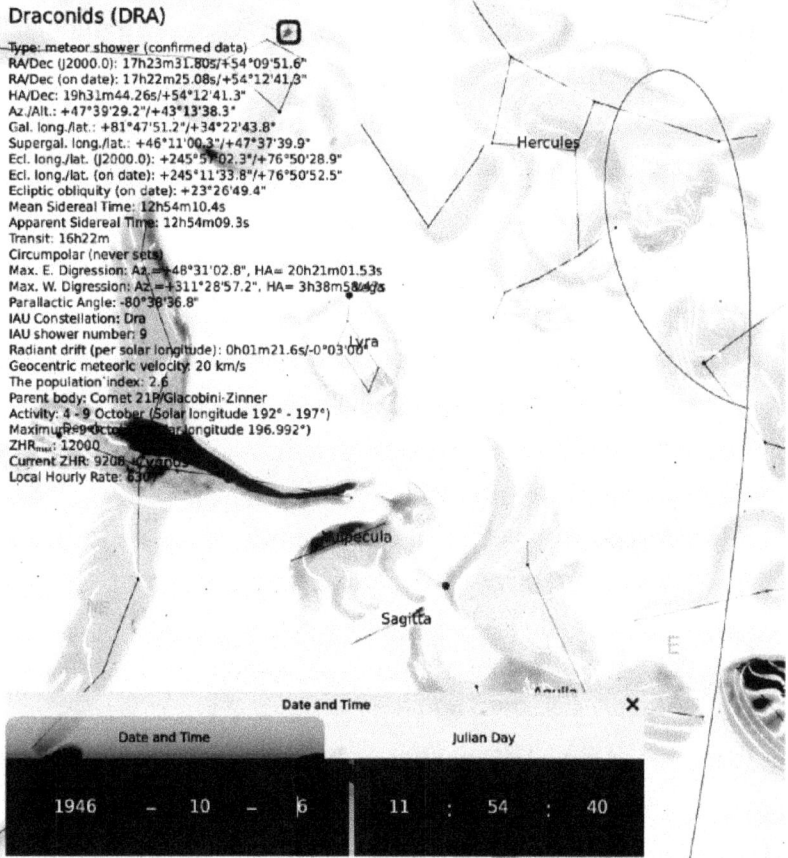

(Source: Stellarium)

9.7 Comets of 1933 and 1946

1933 and 1946 also included the following comet sightings. Comets in Biblical Cosmology can be correlated to wandering stars and "brooms of destruction". Many of these comets were not periodic and may by called "one-hit wonders". These are rare one-apparition comets that appear once in the firmament and do not appear for centuries to millennia.

The six comets found during the year 1933 are as follows :

1. Comet a 1933, discovered by Leslie C. Peltier, of Delphos, Ohio, on February 16.

2. Comet b 1933, a return of the Pons-Winnecke Periodic Comet. It was found by Dr. A. Wachmann at Bergedorf, Germany, on March 24.

3. Comet c 1933, a return of the Giacobini-Zinner Periodic Comet. It was located by Dr. R. Schorr at Bergedorf, Germany, on April 23.

4. Comet d 1933, found by Dr. R. Carrasco at the Madrid Observatory, in Spain, on July 15.

5. Comet e 1933, a return of Wolf's First Periodic Comet. It was found on July 25 by Dr. H. M. Jeffers at the Lick Observatory.

6. Comet / 1933, discovered on October 21, by Dr. F. L. Whipple at the Harvard Observatory. Of the three new and unexpected comets only two, a and f, were well enough observed so that their orbits could be determined. Comet d, found on a double-exposure plate of July 15, was not certainly detected again.[133]

In 1946, several notable comets were observed:

1. The most prominent was Comet Timmers (C/1946 C1), a bright comet discovered in February with a visible tail and a close approach to Earth.

---

[133] https://iopscience.iop.org/article/10.1086/124412/pdf#:~:text=COMET%20MEDAL%20COMMITTEE-,The%20six%20comets%20found%20during%20the%20year%201933%20are%20as,Einarsson

2. Comet Giacobini-Zinner (1946 d) drew attention for its significant brightening and predictions of a strong Draconid meteor shower in October, 1946.

3. Other important discoveries included Comet Jones (1946 h), first seen in the Southern Hemisphere and later visible from the north,

4. Comet Brooks II (1946 e), a faint comet with a slender tail lasting into 1947, and

5. Comet Bester (1946 k), noted in comet reports of the year.

Let's review: Are meteor showers and comets a sign? We know that the Draconids increased to 10,000 and 12,000 meteors per hour in 1933 and 1946. Meteors can be considered falling stars in God's celestial clock. The comets can also be considered falling stars, as they wander into the firmament providing another hand to God's clock. The Mazzaroth signs provide the face of the clock. The path of the comet **21P/Giacobini-Zinner in 1933 and 1946** happens to trace a path of spiritual warfare across the Heavenly clock.

9.8 October and Sukkot

The stars were placed in the Heavens by God for signs and seasons. Seasons are also marked by festivals. The October Draconids are timed around _Sukkot, The Festival of Tabernacles_ where Jewish families follow the custom of building a _sukkah_ (likened to residing with God's loving embrace). In building a sukkah, most people use either palm fronds or bamboo with wooden beams as support. The roof also must be thick enough to provide significant shade, but thin enough to let the _stars shine through_.[134]

---

[134] https://www.ifcj.org/learn/jewish-holidays/what-is-the-festival-of-tabernacles-sukkot

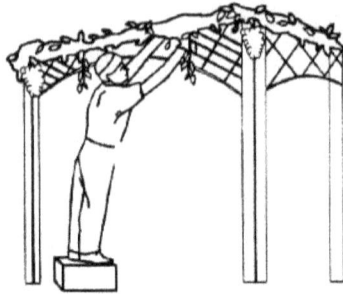

(Source: Clipart Library, Sukkot)[135]

The Sukkot holiday commemorates the exodus of the Jewish people from captivity in Egypt, where they wandered in the wilderness for 40 years. Sukkot is also timed during the autumn harvest. Families will enjoy the celebration with meals within the Sukkot and some family members (especially the men) will sleep in the shelter under the stars.[136]

Let's now look at 2 hypotheses, "educated guesses", based upon the evidence.

9.9 Hypothesis 1: Revelation 6 - The Sixth Seal

Interpretation: Revelation 6:13 may refer to the 2025 Draconid Meteor Shower in temporal proximity to the blood moons of 2025 and solar eclipse of 2024. The 2025 October Draconids are uniquely significant after 2 years (2022 and 2023) of extremely weak showers at ~5 meteors per hour. Also the 2025 meteor showers are stronger at ~400 meteors per hour but not as intense as 1933 and 1946.

> and the **stars of the sky fell to the Earth**, as a fig tree casts its unripe figs when shaken by a great wind.
>
> Revelation 6:13, NASB1995

---

[135] https://clipart-library.com/

[136] https://bje.org.au/knowledge-centre/explained-for-kids/sukkot/

Revelation 6:13 can be broken into the **literal** description of meteor showers: "the stars of the sky fell to Earth" and the **allegorical:** "as a fig tree casts its unripe figs when shaken by a great wind".

9.10 Hypothesis 2: Revelation 12 - The Dragon swept a third of the stars of Heaven... to the Earth.

Interpretation: Revelation 6:13 may refer to the Draconid meteor shower in temporal proximity to the Revelation 12 sign (the woman clothed with the sun and the moon at her feet) on September 23rd, 2017.

The Draconids are in Draco, the dragon, Satan, the serpent of old. In 2018 the comet passed the Earth's plane at a relatively close distance creating a meteor shower which is ~1 year from the September 23rd, 2017 sign. The 2018 October Draconid meteor shower outburst was measured to reach ~100 ZHR, which is less than the 2025 Draconids, but significantly higher than 2022 and 2023.[137]

> "And his [Satan the fiery red dragon's] tail swept away a third of the stars of Heaven and threw them to the Earth."
> (Revelation 12:4, NASB1995)

9.11 Revelation Timeline

The timeline has been updated with two October Draconids 2018 and 2025 (7 years apart - God's perfect number).

---

[137] https://articles.adsabs.harvard.edu//full/2019eMetN...4...74M/0000077.000.html

Fig. 9.11 Revelation 6, 12, & 13 Timeline

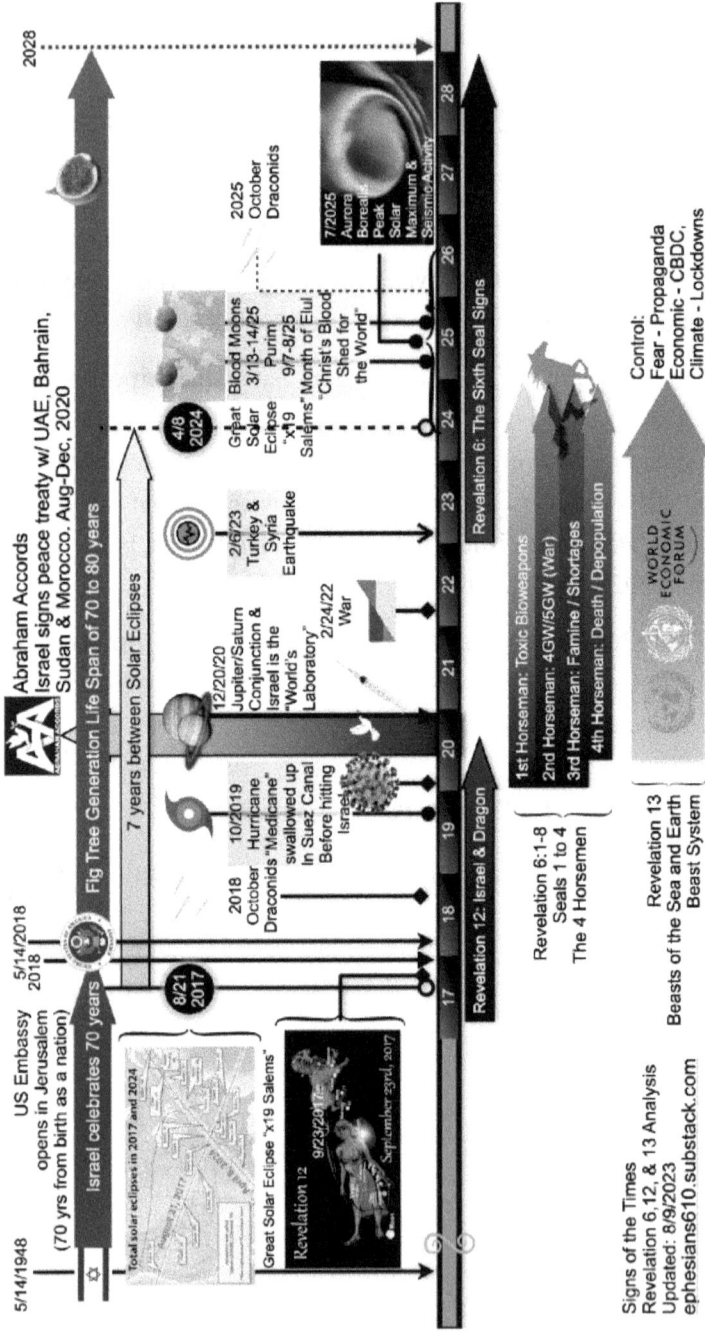

Chapter 10. Unripe Figs Shaken by a Great Wind

In Revelation 6:13, why did Apostle John use the phrase "unripe figs when shaken by a great wind" in this verse?

> and the stars of the sky fell to the Earth, as a fig tree casts its **unripe figs. when shaken by a great wind.** Revelation 6:13, NASB1995

The ESV translation describes the stars as "winter fruit". First, let's research the Greek word *epesan* for "fell".

10.1 Scripture Word Study on "Stars Fell"

Fig. 10.1.1 Interlinear View of Revelation 6:13, ESV

blood,	^{13} and	^{l} the	stars	of the	sky	fell	to	the
αἷμα$_{27}$	καί$_1$	οἱ$_2$	ἀστέρες$_3$ ▶5	τοῦ$_4$	οὐρανοῦ$_5$	ἔπεσαν$_6$	εἰς$_7$	τὴν$_8$
haima	kai	hoi	asteres	tou	ouranou	epesan	eis	tēn
129	2532	3588	792	3588	3772	4098	1519	3588

earth	^{m} as	the	fig	tree	sheds	its	winter
γῆν$_9$	ὡς$_{10}$ →		συκῆ$_{11}$ ←		βάλλει$_{12}$	αὐτῆς$_{15}$	→
gēn	hōs		sykē		ballei	autēs	
1093	5613		4808		906	846	

fruit	when	shaken	by	a	gale	.
τοὺς$_{13}$ ὀλύνθους$_{14}$ →		σειομένη$_{19}$	ὑπὸ$_{16}$ →		ἀνέμου$_{17}$ μεγάλου$_{18}$	
tous olynthous		seiomenē	hypo		anemou megalou	
3588 3653		4579	5259		417 3173	

The "stars of the sky fell" initially paints a picture of meteor showers. The Greek word *epesan* denotes *fail, fall (down), and light on.* These interpretations do vary from the translation of "fell". Apostle John uses *epesan* a total of eight times in the Book of Revelation. The majority of the times John uses *epesan* in context to *bowing down* in worship and once for *nations collapsing*. How does this apply to stars? The interpretation of *epesan* as "light on" could apply to a star. Furthermore, the word *epesan* (Strong's concordance 4098) is related to 4072 *petomai* which denotes to fly, fly(-ing), or the idea of *alighting*. "Light on" and "alighting" seem appropriate for a star.

> 4098. πίπτω piptō, pip´-to; a redupl. and contr. form of πέτω pĕtō, pet´-o (which occurs only as an alt. in cert. tenses); prob. akin to 4072 through the idea of **alighting**; to fall (lit or fig.):— fail, fall (down), **light on**.[138]

In the Bible *alighting* can be symbolic of a bird descending and landing to rest. For example, the Holy Spirit descended as a dove on Jesus at His baptism. The stars "alighted" to the Earth could be a more appropriate interpretation versus the rapid "scary" image of falling stars.

10.2 Scripture Word Study on "Unripe Figs"

Apostle John writes "as the fig tree sheds its winter fruit" in the ESV version or "unripe figs" in the Lexham English Bible. See Strong's Concordance 3653:

> 3653. ὄλυνθος ŏlunthŏs, ol´-oon-thos; of uncert. der.; an unripe (because out of season) fig:—untimely fig.[139]

"Unripe fig" or "winter fruit" in Greek is *olunthos* which denotes an "unripe, out of season, or untimely fig". Scholars believe this usage is to describe an untimely fig, one which, not ripening in due time, grows through the winter and falls off in the spring.[140] Some scholars interpret this as meaning "green figs", symbolizing people unprepared for divine judgement from God's wrath that may come with great force and

---

[138] Strong, J. (2009). In A Concise Dictionary of the Words in the Greek Testament and The Hebrew Bible (Vol. 1, p. 58). Logos Bible Software.

[139] Strong, J. (2009). In A Concise Dictionary of the Words in the Greek Testament and The Hebrew Bible (Vol. 1, p. 51). Logos Bible Software.

[140] https://biblehub.com/greek/3653.htm

overwhelm the unrepentant.[141] This interpretation may be valid symbolically, however, let's continue to dig deeper. Let's remember that the Revelation 6, Sixth Seal signs, are describing a series of astronomical and seismic events.

Why is the word *olunthos* only used **once** through the entire Bible?

Why would Apostle John use this word specifically to describe the stars that fell or "alighted" like a bird with wings?

For example, the word for fig, the fruit, in Greek is *sukon* (Strong's Concordance 4810)[142] and not *olunthos* (Strong's Concordance 3653).

> 4808. συκῆ sukē, soo-kay´; from 4810; a fig-tree:—fig tree.[143]
>
> 4810. σῦκον sukŏn, soo´-kon; appar. a prim. word; a fig:—fig.[144]

So why did John use the term *olunthos* vs *sukon?*

Was he trying to provide a visual description of unripe figs that are very difficult to fall off the tree, thus only blowing off when there is a great wind? Was he trying to describe a very rare celestial event, possibly equating unripe figs, or winter fruit, to rare meteor storm outbursts, or rare comets?

In the original 2023 version of this book, it was proposed that there was a rare cosmic event, where great forces would cause meteor storms to fall from Heaven. It was originally proposed that this was a rare planetary alignment with a comet which would increase dust particles that caused an outburst of meteors. However, now in 2025, we can look back to better assess what was meant by the unique Biblical use of *olunthos,* denoting an

---

[141] https://biblehub.com/greek/3653.htm

[142] https://biblehub.com/greek/4810.htm

[143] Strong, J. (2009). In A Concise Dictionary of the Words in the Greek Testament and The Hebrew Bible (Vol. 1, p. 67). Logos Bible Software.

[144] Strong, J. (2009). In A Concise Dictionary of the Words in the Greek Testament and The Hebrew Bible (Vol. 1, p. 68). Logos Bible Software.

unripe fig, or rare star. Is this what Apostle John was trying to convey in Revelation 6:13 - a rare series of comets?

Fig. 10.2.1 Engraving of Comets as Wandering Stars

(Source: public domain)

Fig. 10.1.1 is an engraving depicting some of the most famous comets over the centuries: Halley's Comet (1835), Donatis Comet (1858), and comets of 1680, 1741, and 1811 (artist unknown, ca. 1860). Comets tend to wander from the great expanse into the firmament. Some are periodic and some only visit once, never to be seen again. Some travel along the ecliptic with the sun, moon, and planets. Others wander all over the Mazzaroth and do not follow the ecliptic.

From 2017 to 2025 there have been more than one rare wandering star, or "once in a lifetime" comet, that has traveled into the firmament to pass through and suddenly "light on" and "alight" the Earth. Let's analyze some of these comets.

10.3 The 2018 & 2025 Comet Paths

Fig. 10.3.1 Comet 21P Path in 2018

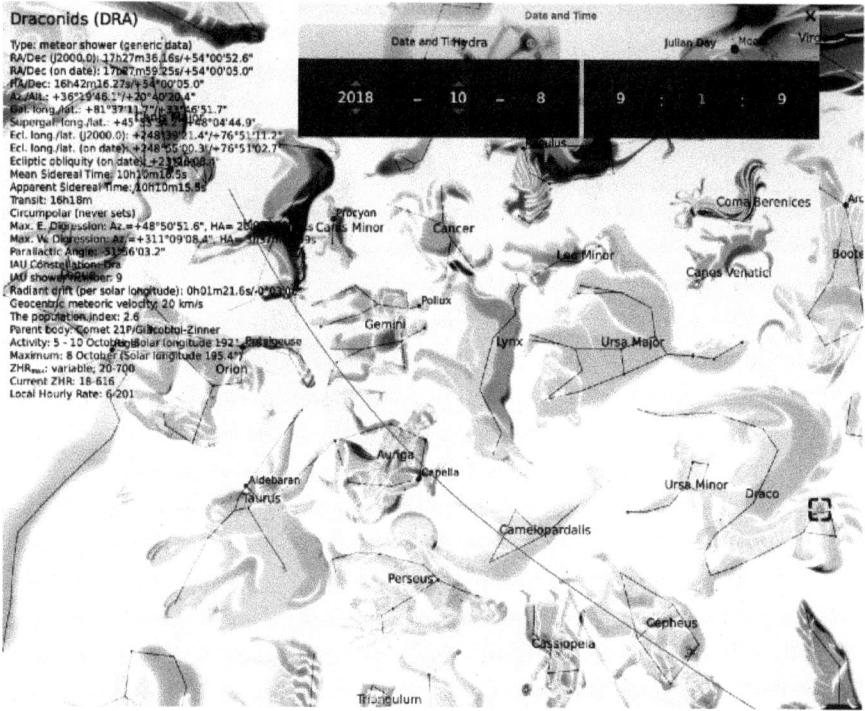

(Source: Stellarium)

In Fig. 10.3.1 and Fig 10.3.2, the path of **comet 21P/Giacobini-Zinner** did not circle Hercules and the three-headed Hydra as in 1933 and 1946. The paths do not make a loop as in Fig 9.6.1 and Fig. 9.6.2, but take an arc cutting through the ecliptic that follows Taurus, Gemini, Cancer, and Leo (from bottom-left to top-right).

In Fig. 10.3.1, the 2018 path starts in Cepheus to Auriga. Then it travels between Taurus and Pleiades, the seven stars, to Gemini and Orion.

In Fig. 10.3.2, the 2025 path starts in Pisces and breaks the chord between the fish and Cetus, the Beast of the Sea (Revelation 13). The wandering star then flies between Orion and Taurus with the Pleiades, the seven stars in the Book of Revelation associated with the angels and seven churches. Then 21P travels directly into Hydra the crooked serpent in the top-left of Fig. 10.3.2, bisecting the head of the serpent of old, Satan.

Fig. 10.3.2 Comet 21P Path in 2025

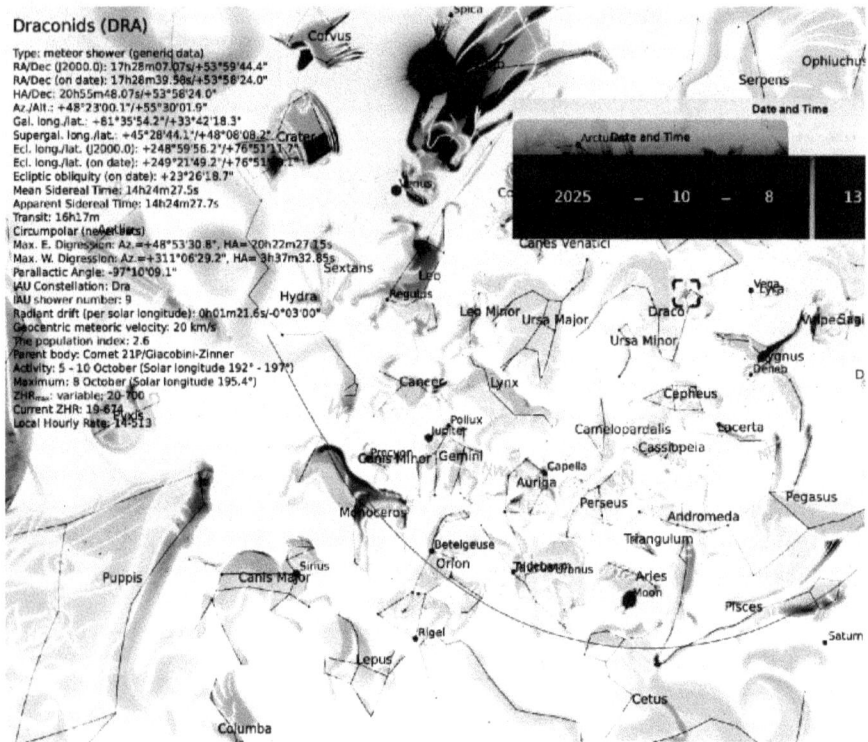

(Source: Stellarium)

Common in both 2018 and 2025 paths are the constellations called out by God in the Book of Job and Amos.

> who made the Bear and **Orion, the Pleiades** and the chambers of the south; Job 9:9[145]
>
> "Can you **bind the chains of the Pleiades or loose the cords of Orion**?
>
> Can you lead forth the **Mazzaroth** in their season, or can you guide the Bear with its children?

---

[145] The Holy Bible: English Standard Version (Job 9:9). (2016). Crossway Bibles.

> Do you know the ordinances of the heavens? Can you establish their rule on the earth? Job 38:31–33[146]

> He who made the **Pleiades and Orion**, and turns deep darkness into the morning and darkens the day into night, who calls for the waters of the sea and pours them out on the surface of the earth, the LORD is his name; Amos 5:8[147]

If **comet 21P/Giacobini-Zinner** was the only comet during this window of time, it would already be notable in this book as evidence of rare events, however **comet 21P/Giacobini-Zinner** is periodic and has a cadence of just under 7 years. 21P does bookend a window of time from 2018 to 2025 where other very rare comets have been discovered.

10.4 Notable Comets between 2017 and 2025

Let's review the meteor shower outbursts as they relate to comets. Astronomers believe the Draconid meteor showers are remains of the **comet 21P/Giacobini-Zinner, a periodic comet.** In 2025 the Draconids peaked on October 8th, 2025 to ~400 ZHR which was not as great as 1933 and 1946. The 2018 Draconids reached ~100 ZHR. Both 2018 and 2025 Draconids came from the eye of the dragon, Draco. Both meteor showers bookended a period of time with rare comet discoveries.

Stepping back, what if *olunthos* denoting unripe figs meant rare comets? What if Apostle John saw in his vision rare wandering stars? What are some of these rare comets?

Mainstream Media has been buzzing in this window of time about a series of rare wandering interstellar visitors. These visitors are very rare in that they are not periodic, and in some cases they do not seem to even behave like a comet. They are considered interstellar visitors to our neighborhood in the firmament.

---

[146] The Holy Bible: English Standard Version (Job 38:31–33). (2016). Crossway Bibles.

[147] The Holy Bible: English Standard Version (Am 5:8). (2016). Crossway Bibles.

Table. 10.4.1 Rare Interstellar Non-Periodic Visitors 2017 to 2025

Interstellar Object	Discovered	Description
1I/'Oumuamua	2017	First interstellar object discovered entering Earth's firmament October 2017. It had an elongated shape and lacked a traditional comet tail.
2I/Borisov	2019	Second interstellar object discovered which did have a coma and tail like a comet.
3I/ATLAS	2025	Third interstellar object discovered July 2025. It had a nickel composition and started to turn green as it approached Earth. It's closest approach to earth was December 2025.

Table 10.4.1 lists three interstellar objects which were discovered in 2017, 2019, and 2025. **All three were never seen before and appeared relatively suddenly.**

On Oct. 19, 2017, shortly after the Revelation 12 sign of September 23rd, 2017, astronomers discovered an odd-shaped comet or asteroid, and they gave it the name 1I/'Oumuamua (pronounced oh MOO-uh MOO-uh), which is Hawai'ian for "a messenger from afar arriving first." It was the first of its kind ever discovered. Oumuamua had the shape of a long cigar and was located in the constellation of Virgo the Virgin.

A couple of years later, in the constellation of Leo the Lion, 2I/Borisov was discovered by Gennady Borisov and given the indicator "2I", which signified the 2nd Interstellar visitor. Neither had a fuzzy coma glow nor a tail like a typical comet.

In 2025, the 3rd Interstellar object was discovered by the Asteroid Terrestrial-impact Last Alert System (ATLAS) and was closest to Earth on December 19th, 2025. 3I/ATLAS passed over Virgo and Leo the Lion.

In addition to these "Interstellar visitors", many other comets were documented. Table 10.4.2 is not an exhaustive list yet it shows an impressive number of long period comets, especially those that have an estimated orbit of tens of thousands of years.

Table. 10.4.2 Comets with Orbits from 2018 to 2025

Comet	Orbit	Sighted	Description
46P/Wirtanen	5.4 yrs	2018	"Christmas Comet" close Earth pass on December 2018
21P/Giacobini-Zinner	6.6 yrs	2018	Source of the Draconid meteor showers. It passed near the sun in 2018 and then the next significant return is 2031.
C/2020 F3 (NEOWISE)	6,800 yrs	2020	NEOWISE became a "grand show" that exceeded expectations. It was easily visible to the naked eye for observers in the Northern Hemisphere and produced stunning photos, becoming one of the top comets in decades.
C/2021 A1 (Leonard)	80,000 yrs	2021	Brightest comet of 2021; disintegrated near the sun.
C/2017 K2 (PANSTARRS)	3 to 4 million yrs	2022	A long-period comet observed as it approached in December 2022.
C/2022 E3 (ZTF)	50,000 yrs	2022	"The Green Comet" The Green Comet will be at its closest point to Earth, and will be brightest in our skies, on February 1st, 2023, within one week of the Great Earthquake in Turkey and Syria on February 6th, 2023.
C/2023 A3 (Tsuchinshan - ATLAS)	80,000 yrs	2024	"Comet of the Century" Visible in the Northern Hemisphere with the naked eye as it circled Virgo from the head to the foot. ~80k year orbit

Comet	Orbit	Sighted	Description
13P/Olbers	69 yrs	2024	Earth-based observers were able to view the comet in mid-July 2024, and its next return projected for 2094.
12P/Pons-Brooks	71 yrs	2024	A Halley-type periodic comet with a 71-year orbital period, it made a much-anticipated return and was visible in early 2024, sometimes exhibiting a distinctive "horned" appearance due to outbursts
C/2025 A6 Lemmon	1350 yrs	2025	The Comet is near Scorpius on December 22nd, 2025
C/2024 G3 (ATLAS)	160,000 yrs	2025	"New Year's Comet" with ~160k year orbit. Was visible near Sagittarius.

10.5 Hypothesis 3: Revelation 6 - Rare Comets

Revelation 6:13 may refer to rare comets. Comets are suddenly discovered, "light on", like wandering stars that fly through the firmament. Comets are like winter fruit, unripe figs, or birds descending from Heaven as if they were blown in from the great expanse. Comets descend, "alight"[148], like celestial "angels" (Job 38:7) and some are associated to seismic events, or "brooms of destruction" (Isaiah 14:23).

[148] https://biblehub.com/greek/4098.htm

Chapter 11. Probability of Comets and Mazzaroth Paths

Let's continue this study of "wandering stars", statistics, and scripture to build up the perseverance of the saints. This Chapter has been updated to focus on the mathematical probability of comets and also supernatural paths of the comets through the Mazzaroth which seem to follow Scripture as a series of "signs". This Chapter will build upon the previous hypotheses numbered 1 to 3 (see: Section 9.10, 9.11, and 10.5).

11.1 The Draconid Meteor Shower from Draco

First let's revisit the 21P/Giacobini-Zinner comet, producing meteor showers on Earth, which radiate from the constellation Draco, called the October Draconids. Sometimes it's a trickle of 5 meteors per hour… but on very rare occasion, it's a storm of 10,000 per hour. What's the probability that in 2025 it will be a meteor storm blown by a great gravitational solar wind?

With the Draconids producing comet, 21P/Giacobini-Zinner, the letter "P" indicates that Giacobini-Zinner is a periodic comet. Periodic comets have an orbital period of **less than 200 years**.[149]

The orbit of 21P is **6.62** years = 1/6.62

11.2 Combined Probability with A Periodic Comet

Therefore, what is the probability of the Earthquake and aftershock, solar eclipses, lunar eclipses where the whole moon became like blood for

---

[149] https://solarsystem.nasa.gov/asteroids-comets-and-meteors/comets/21p-giacobini-zinner/in-depth/

all the nations to see, and the Draconids meteor shower? The probability of previous Sixth Seal signs and a periodic comet of 6.62 years

= 1/(2.6592e+12 x 6.62) = 1/1.7603904e+13

= one over seventeen trillion six hundred three billion nine hundred four million

= 5.6805581e-14

= 0.000000000000056805581

A zero probability is an impossible event. A probability of 1 is a certain event. A number of 5.6805581e-14 is very close to zero so a very unlikely event.

11.3 Combined Probability with Rare Comets

Now when one factors in the "Interstellar visitors" of Table 10.4.1, it becomes even more impossible. These wandering stars have never been recorded before on Earth. Attempting to calculate the probability of 1I/'Oumuamua, 2I/Borisov, and 3I/ATLAS are literally impossible.

However, we can attempt to factor in the comets of Table 10.4.2. since we are given an estimated orbit of each comet in years. Let's use the long period comets. The estimated probability of the listed long period comets occurring in Table 10.4.2 are,

= 1/(6.8k x 18k x 3M x 50k x 80k x 160k yrs) = 1/2.35008e+29
= 4.2551743e-30

Combine this with the previous probability,

= 5.6805581e-14 x 4.2551743e-30 = 2.4171765e-43 = which is basically zero.

11.4 Interstellar Paths Through The Mazzaroth

Let's take a look at the rare "Interstellar visitors" again, but from a Heavenly sign perspective. One interstellar object being sighted is a rare occurrence alone, but three within seven years reaches levels of being impossible. Are these wandering stars for signs and seasons? Were they created by God for an appointed time to give mankind a message? Are the Heavens to proclaim His glory?

Fig. 11.4.1 Comet 1I/'Oumuamua 2017 Mazzaroth Origin

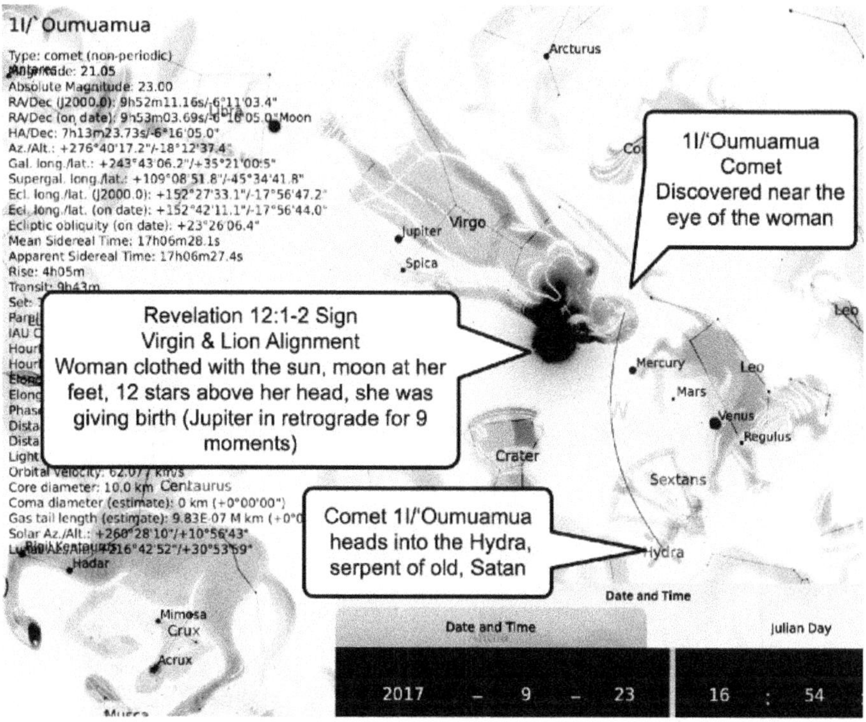

In Fig. 11.4.1, the first interstellar object, 1I/'Oumuamua, is plotted against the Mazzaroth. It was discovered at the time of the September 23rd, 2017 Revelation 12 sign. The path of 1I/'Oumuamua passes near the eye of the woman, Virgo, shortly before the Revelation 12 alignment of the sun clothing the woman with the moon at her feet and 12 stars above her head. Jupiter was in retrograde motion in the womb of the woman. 1I/'Oumuamua moves away from the woman and Leo the Lion to Hydra, the crooked serpent, the serpent of old, Satan.

Fig. 11.4.2 Comet 1I/'Oumuamua 2017 Mazzaroth Full Path

In Fig. 11.4.2, the path of 1I/'Oumuamua continues to "decapitate" the head of the Hydra, it then travels along the belt of Orion past the star Mintaka, denoting dividing as a sacrifice. The 1I/'Oumuamua object continues to "decapitate" Cetus, the Beast of the Sea. Then the object 1I/'Oumuamua continues to Pisces, and its star Alsamaca, denoting the upheld.

Was 1I/'Oumuamua foreshadowing the coming spiritual battle? 2017 to 2019 was a relative period of prosperity and peace. However, the Beast of the Sea, Cetus, was given authority by the dragon, the serpent of old, Satan (Revelation 12 and 13). The fiery red dragon, serpent of old, Satan is symbolized by both Hydra, the crooked serpent, or Draco, the dragon.

Fig. 11.4.3 Comet 2I/Borisov 2019 Near Regulus

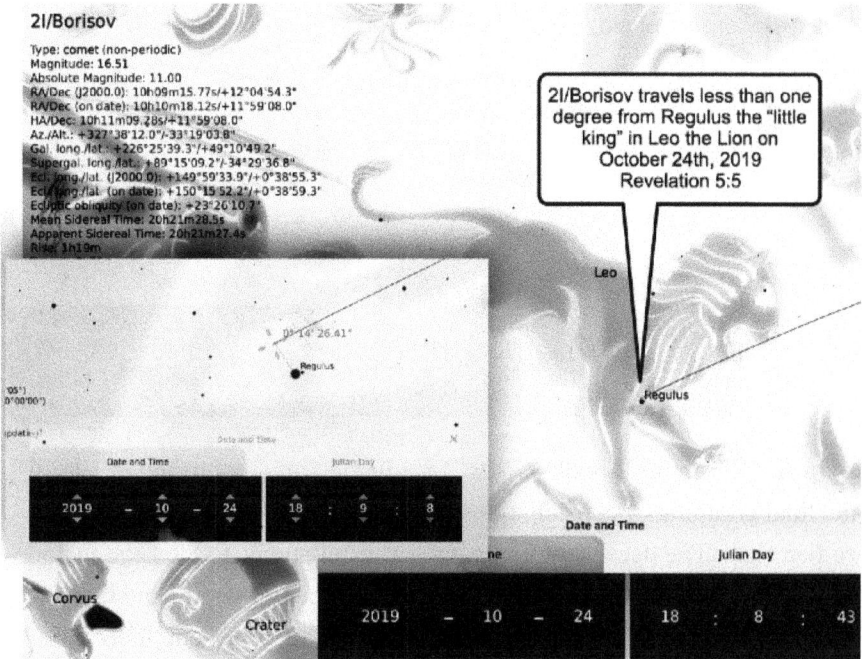

Fig. 11.4.4 Comet 2I/Borisov 2019 Full Path

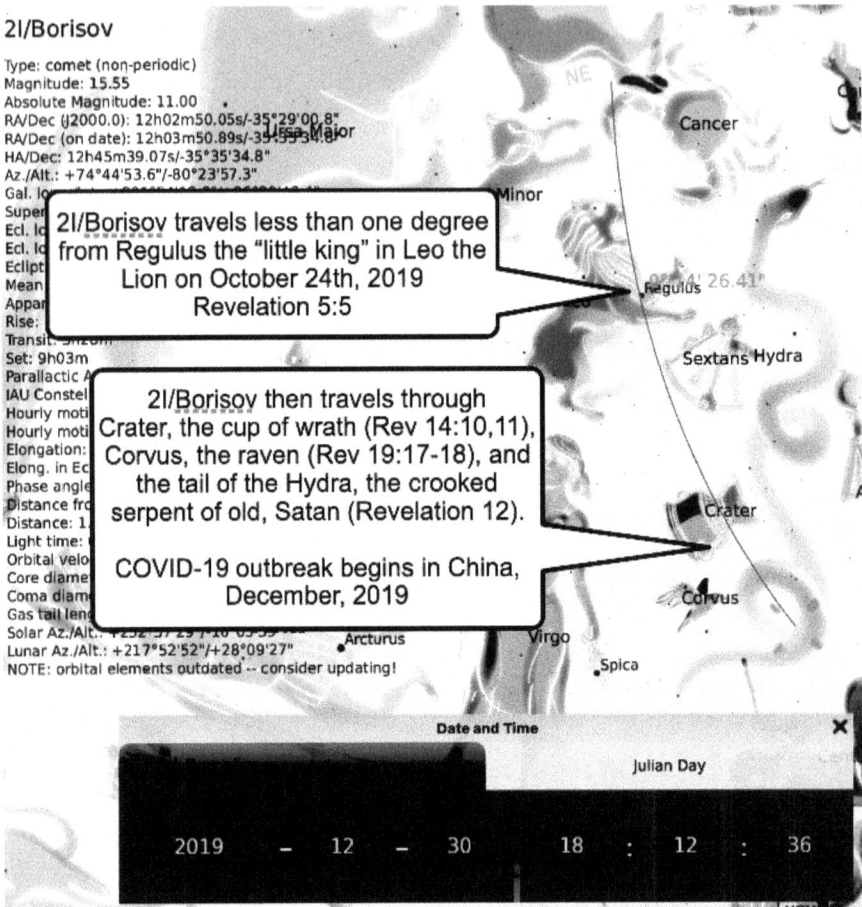

In K. C. Fleming's book, *God's Voice in the Stars*, published in 1981[150], the final grouping of constellations centers on Leo the Lion, the twelfth zodiac sign. The decans, or companion constellations, to the Lion include Hydra the crooked serpent, Crater, the bowl or cup of wrath, and Corvus, the bird, or raven. The four constellations together represent "Leo, His Enemies Destroyed, Christ the Victor"[151].

---

[150] Fleming, K. C. *God's Voice in the Stars*, Loizeaux Brothers, Neptune, New Jersey, 1981

[151] https://mazzarothgospel.blogspot.com/

The 2nd interstellar comet, 2I/Borisov, starts in Leo the Lion. In Fig. 11.4.3, 2I/Borisov travels within less than one degree from Regulus the "little king" in Leo the Lion on October 24th, 2019.

> 5 And one of the elders said to me, "Weep no more; behold, the Lion of the tribe of Judah, the Root of David, has conquered, so that he can open the scroll and its seven seals." Revelation 5:5, ESV[152]

In Fig. 11.4.4, 2I/Borisov travels from the Lion of Judah to Crater, the cup of divine wrath (see Revelation 14:10), Corvus, the raven, and the tail of the Hydra, the serpent of old, Satan. Each Mazzaroth sign brings forth Scripture. Leo the Lion in the Book of Revelation represents Jesus Christ who destroys His enemies. In the Book of Revelation, Chapter 14, an angel warns mankind not to worship the Beast of the Sea from Chapter 13.

> "If anyone worships the beast and its image and receives a mark on his forehead or on his hand he also will drink the wine of God's wrath, poured full strength into the **cup of his anger**, and he will be tormented with fire and sulfur in the presence of the holy angels and in the presence of the Lamb." Revelation 14:10, ESV[153]

Then in Chapter 19, the King of Kings, Jesus Christ, on a white horse brings His Wrath on the Beast and His demonic armies which are gorged upon by the birds, ravens.

> And the rest were slain by the sword that came from the mouth of him who was sitting on the horse, and all the **birds** were gorged with their flesh. Revelation 19:21, ESV[154]

Then 2I/Borisov, crosses the Hydra's tail, the ancient crooked serpent during the month of December, 2019, when the COVID-19 outbreak begins in China.

---

152 The Holy Bible: English Standard Version (Re 5:5). (2025). Crossway Bibles.

153The Holy Bible: English Standard Version (Re 14:10). (2025). Crossway Bibles.

154 The Holy Bible: English Standard Version (Re 19:21). (2025). Crossway Bibles.

And he seized the **dragon, that ancient serpent,** who is the devil and Satan, and bound him for a thousand years, 3 and threw him into the pit, and shut it and sealed it over him, so that he might not deceive the nations any longer, until the thousand years were ended. After that he must be released for a little while. Revelation 20:2–3, ESV[155]

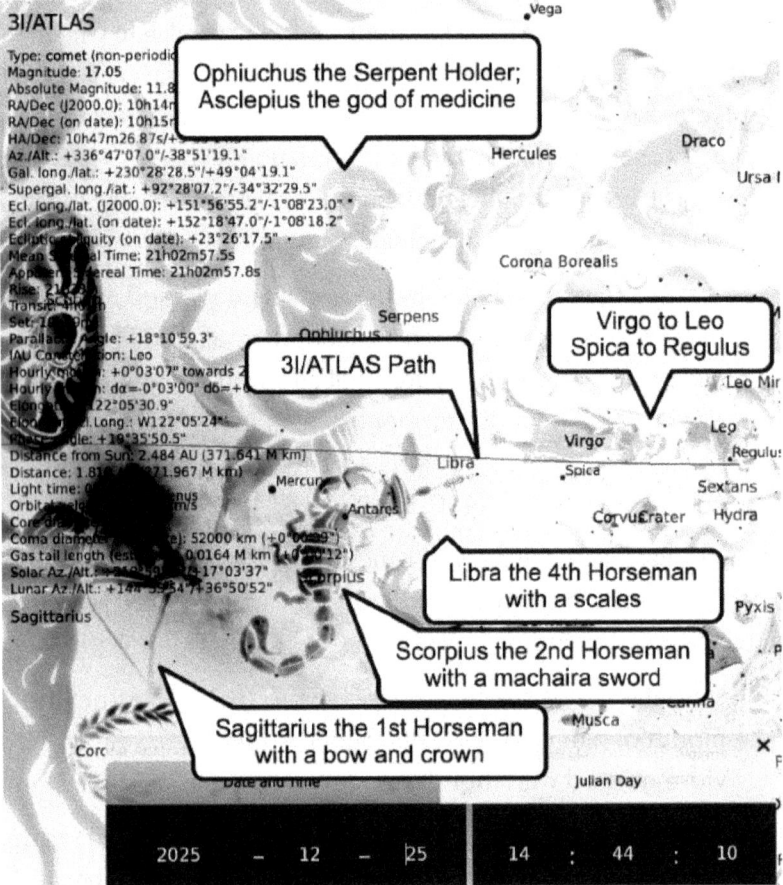

Fig. 11.4.5 Comet 3I/ATLAS 2025

In Fig. 11.4.5, 3I/ATLAS makes its first and final pass to Earth. The comet is discovered above Sagittarius the First Horseman, who holds a bow and has a crown, Corona Australis at its foot. Then 3I/ATLAS travels

---

155 The Holy Bible: English Standard Version (Re 20:2–3). (2025). Crossway Bibles.

above Scorpius, the Second Horseman with a machaira sword tail. Then the comet travels through Libra, the Third Horseman with a pair of scales.

The rare visitor then connects Spica to Regulus. The Seed of the Woman to the Little King in the Lion of Judah. By traveling through Virgo and Leo, the wandering star passes through the same two constellations described in the Revelation 12:1-2 great sign in Heaven.

Fig. 11.4.6 Comet 3I/ATLAS Spica to Regulus

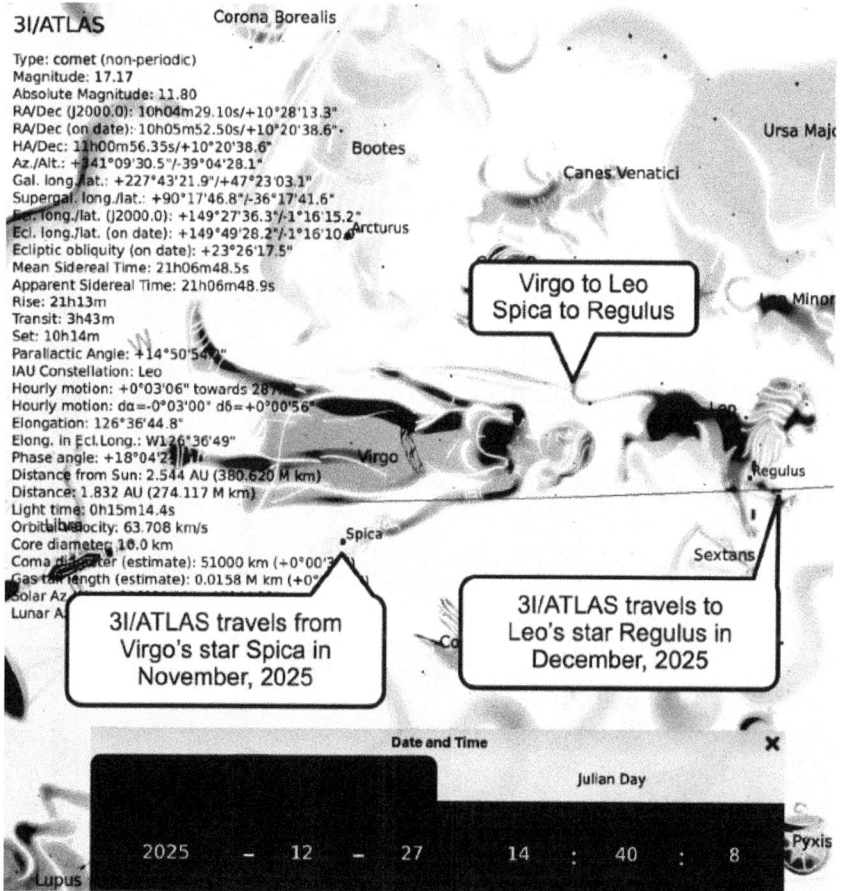

Fig. 11.4.7 Interstellar Visitors Timeline

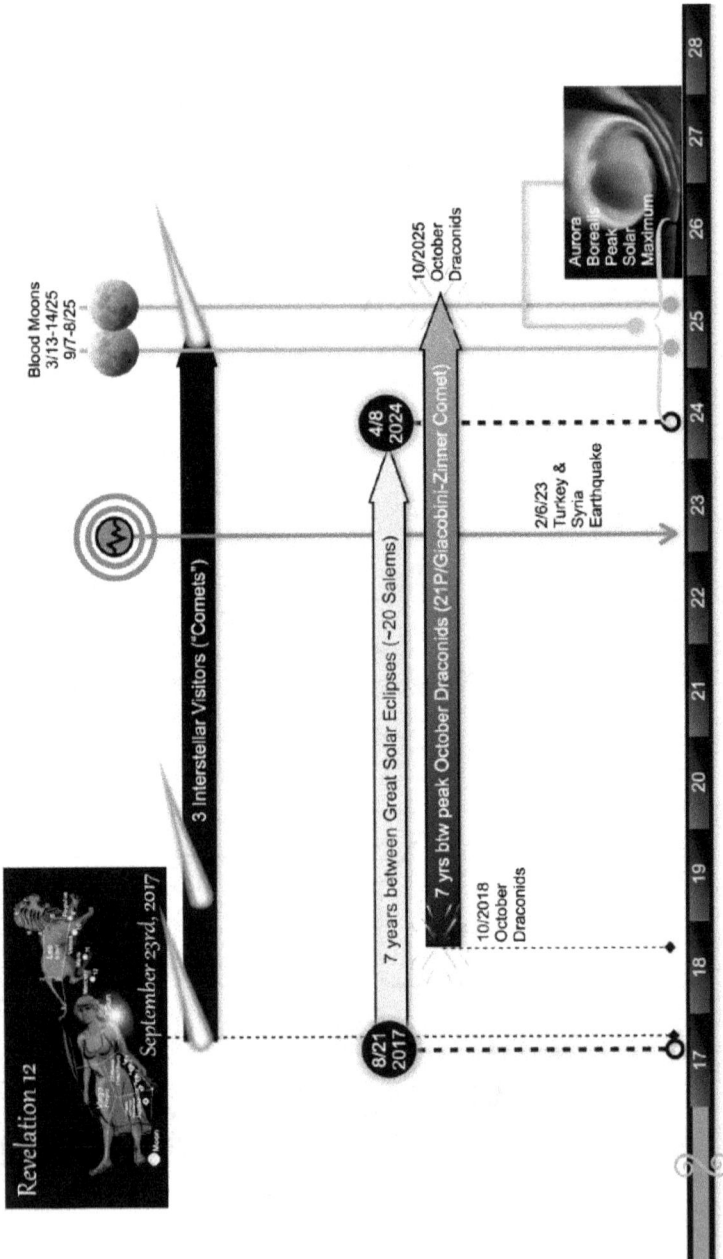

11.5 Comet Sighted By Author

Introducing a once in a lifetime passing of comet C/2023 A3 (Tsuchinshan-ATLAS). Astronomers have already named it the "Comet of the Century". On October 18th, 2024, "The Deceiving Dragon Comets and the Cup of God's Divine Wrath" was published by myself,

> I captured the following two photographs on Wednesday, October 17th, 2024. Rising in the East through the trees was the largest supermoon of 2024 and following the setting sun in the West was the "Comet of the Century" C/2023 A3 (Tshuchinshan-ATLAS). My eyes had to adjust from the moon's brightness to the comet's faintness using Venus (to the left) and Arcturus (to the right) as reference points to locate the comet. The comet reminded me of a *boiling pot or kettle spewing steam* (Jeremiah 1:13–19).[156]

Fig. 11.4.8 Supermoon and Comet C/2023 A3

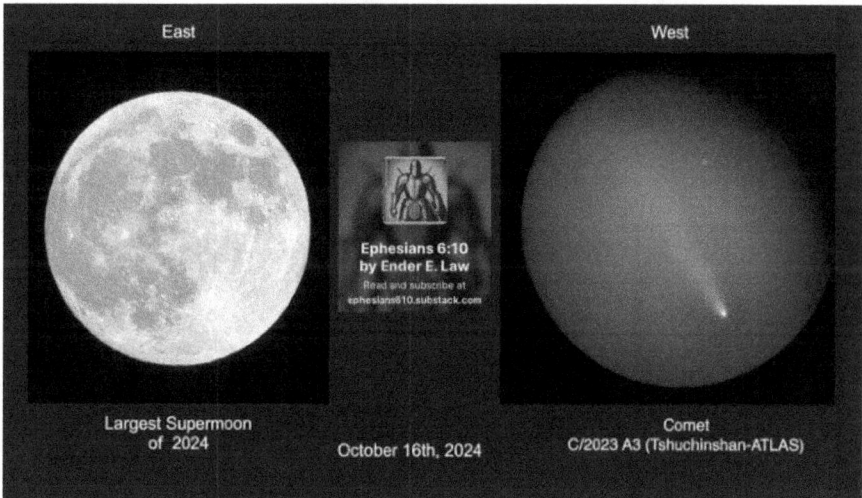

On October 14th, 2024, 13P/Olbers will have a very rare conjunction with comet C/2023 A3 (Tsuchinshan-ATLAS) at Virgo the Virgin. Comet A3 was discovered February 2023 by astronomers at both South Africa's

---

[156] https://ephesians610.substack.com/p/the-deceiving-dragon-comets-and-the

Asteroid Terrestrial-impact Last Alert System (ATLAS) telescope and China's Tsuchinshan Observatory.[157] C/2023 A3 (Tsuchinshan-ATLAS) has an **80k-year orbit** of the sun so mathematically this comet has never been seen since the Biblical Creation.

On October 15th, 2024, the "Comet of the Century" C/2023 A3 (Tshuchinshan-ATLAS), is shown below at the feet of the virgin. Yet not visible to the human eye is the comet 13P/Olbers within 1 degree of separation from the "Comet of the Century", like a cosmic hand-off. The probability of C/2023 A3 and 13P orbiting the sun in the same year is calculated below:

$$1/80,000 \times 1/69 = 1/5,520,000 = 1.8115942e\text{-}7$$

Another mathematical impossibility of "unripe figs" or "winter fruit" that suddenly "light on" and "alight" the Earth between 2017 and 2025.

Fig. 11.5.1 Comet 13P/Olbers and C/2023 A3 at Virgo

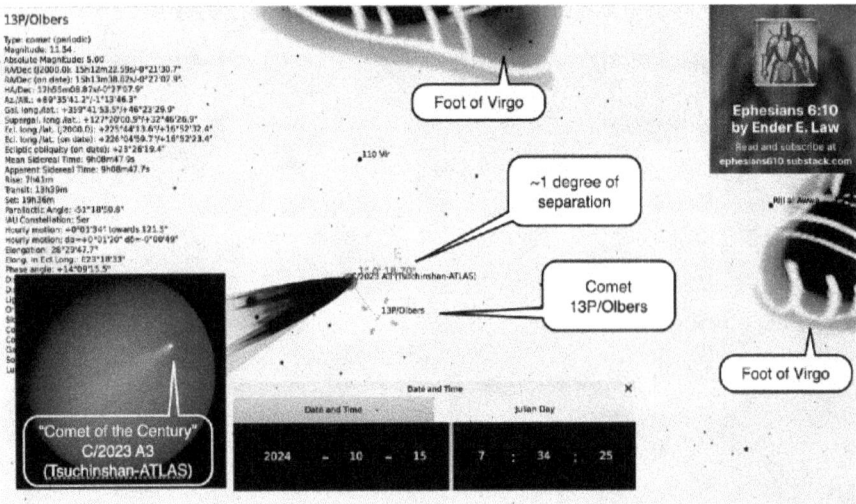

11.6 In Summary

To summarize the three hypotheses:

157 https://www.forbes.com/sites/jamiecartereurope/2024/05/25/saw-the-eclipse-and-aurora-now-comes-a-third-once-in-a-lifetime-event/

Hypothesis 1: Revelation 6:13 of the Sixth Seal can be interpreted as the 2025 Draconid Meteor Shower in temporal proximity to the blood moons of 2025 and solar eclipse of 2024. The 2025 meteor showers resulted ~20 to 500 meteors per hour, but was not as intense as 1933 and 1946 which exceeded 10,000 meteors per hour. This was the initial hypothesis written in the 2023 version of this book and we can now look back on the actual meteor showers which did not become a storm.

Hypothesis 2: In Revelation 12, the fiery red dragon swept a third of the stars of Heaven to the Earth has traditionally been interpreted as fallen angels. In the first version of this book, the October 2018 Draconid meteor shower following the Revelation 12 sign on September 23rd, 2017 was postulated as a possible literal interpretation.

Hypothesis 3: In the revised book, Revelation 6:13 may refer to rare comets. Comets are suddenly discovered, "light on", like wandering stars that fly through the firmament. Comets are like winter fruit, unripe figs, or birds descending from Heaven as if they were blown in from the great expanse. Comets descend, "alight"[158], like celestial "angels" (Job 38:7) and some are associated to seismic events, or "brooms of destruction" (Isaiah 14:23).

In Hypothesis 3, the additional paths of the comets have been analyzed both in this book and on Substack. Probabilities of these signs have been calculated where possible. The comets, "wandering stars", or "brooms of destruction" trace paths through the Heavenly signs to reveal Biblical themes as prophesied by Apostle John in the Book of Revelation and they are extremely rare to the point of being mathematically impossible.

---

[158] https://biblehub.com/greek/4098.htm

Chapter 12. Are the Heavenly Northern Lights a Sign?

14 The sky was split apart like a scroll when it is rolled up (Revelation 6:14a; NASB1995)

There have been many interpretations of this verse from atomic blasts, to a near Earth orbit, to storms… for years many have been in the "I don't know, and time will tell" camp.

We've been studying God's prophetic clock and we have seen how God controls the cycles of the signs in the sun, moon, and stars.

Did you know that God created the sun with an internal clock?

We'll review solar activity cycles, pole shifts, and coronal mass ejections (or **CMEs**) that cause geomagnetic storms and northern lights… we'll also look at the original Greek and the mindset of John as he tried to describe what he saw in the vision of the future.

As I dug into this further I was in awe of God's amazing and beautiful timepiece and I truly hope you enjoy this journey of discovery through the creator of the Earth and Heavens. I also hope that someday you are blessed to look up and see the northern lights very very soon as I plan to do with my wife and children.

This is a continuation of the Revelation Sixth Seal analysis where we have analyzed two Earthquakes, three solar eclipses, two blood moons, and two pairs of meteor showers, and a series of rare and periodic comets

Next up: the northern lights or aurora borealis, which are being sighted much more frequently because of the solar maximum which peaks in 2025.

One can only dream of seeing the northern lights but it seems they are moving south for millions to experience which inspired an unveiling correlation to Revelation 6:14a.

> A phenomenon in the Heavenly skies where the sky is decorated with colorful crepe-paper streamers of green, pink, blue, and red, while uncoiling, curling, and blowing in a gentle breeze as if God is putting on a party.

12.1 Word Study on Revelation 6:14a

Let's start first by analyzing Revelation 6:14a in detail across several Bible translations:

> 14 The sky was split apart like a scroll when it is rolled up (Revelation 6:14a; NASB1995)

> 14 The sky was split [separated from the land] and rolled up like a scroll (Revelation 6:14a; AMP)

> 14 And Heaven went away, as a book wrapped in [or enfolded] (Revelation 6:14a; Wycliff's Bible with Modern Spelling)

> 14 The sky receded like a scroll being rolled up (Revelation 6:14a; Berean Study Bible)

> 14 And Shomayim split apart as a megillah scroll being rolled up (Revelation 6:14a; The Orthodox Jewish Bible)

When aligning these different translations side-by-side, it provides a greater appreciation for the challenging job of translating the ancient Greek language. Let's break this down.

- *ouranos* (Greek) is translated as the Heavens, the sky, the **starry Heavens**, the visible Heavens, or the spiritual Heavens. In Hebrew the word is *Shomayim* meaning the Gates of Heaven or Heavens, where God dwells, with other Heavenly beings, His divine council.[159] In the context

---

[159] https://biblehub.com/text/revelation/6-14.htm

of Second Temple Judaism, Apostle John would look up at the Heavens as the "Unseen Realm" of God and His divine council, as described by the late Dr. Michael Heiser, Old Testament bible scholar. Let's do a word study of each of the key words in Revelation 6:14a using Biblehub.com:

• *apochórizó, or apechōristhē* (Greek) means to separate, "**part asunder**". It's translated as "split apart, receded, separated from the land, departed, and went away". It is only used twice in the entire bible. *apochórizó* is used once here in Revelation 6 and another time in Acts 15:39 to describe how Paul and Barnabus had a disagreement and parted.[160]

• *biblion* (Greek) means a **paper or book**. It is only translated as a scroll once in Revelation but used over 900 times in the bible and most often translated as book as well as certificate. In Hebrew, *megillah* is scroll.

• *helissomenon, or helissó* (Greek) means to **roll or coil**. The word is only used twice in the entire Bible, once here in Revelation 6 and another time in Hebrews 1:12 to describe rolling a robe or mantle (i.e.: a loose cloth covering such as a cloak or shawl).[161]

12.2 What did John See?

Apostle John, the cousin of Jesus, authored New Testament books of *John, Revelation, 1st, 2nd, and 3rd John*. What did he see when he wrote this verse? What is the *exogesis*[162]? Or in simpler terms, what is the allegorical picture "leading out" of this verse? First we have to try and put ourselves into the historical context of the writer.

---

[160] https://biblehub.com/greek/673.htm

[161] https://biblehub.com/greek/1667.htm

[162] https://seminary.grace.edu/what-is-biblical-hermeneutics/
#:~:text=Where%20exegesis%20refers%20to%20the,order%20to%20interpret%20the%20text.

Apostle John, the last living disciple of Jesus, would have been writing with ink on parchment… rolling/unrolling sheets, pages curling, and attempting to keep each sheet from moving, using a paper weight in order to keep pages flat. He would be careful to capture every Greek character properly without any mistakes using permanent ink. Once John lifts the paper weight the curled pages would roll together again, and he would need to patiently repeat the process on a new piece of parchment.

Fig. 12.2.1 Scroll on Parchment

The Apostle John is banished to the island of Patmos and is given this vision of an astronomical sign to document, and in historical context of his Second Temple Judaism world, he sees this awesome sign in Heaven and attempts to describe it. How can one describe this awesome spectacle in the sky?

Maybe John was reminded of something he was familiar with. He looks up and sees the ribbons of light curling, rolling, and unfolding before his eyes. He looks down transcribing the words of Jesus onto unrolled pages of parchment by flickering candlelight. He finished the letters to the seven churches of Revelation and sent them out in scrolls of parchment. The image is fresh in his mind and it fits… he describes this Heavenly sight using the allegorical picture of what he is holding in his hands. Is this a possible interpretation of what John saw?

Fig. 12.2.2 Northern Lights and Scrolls

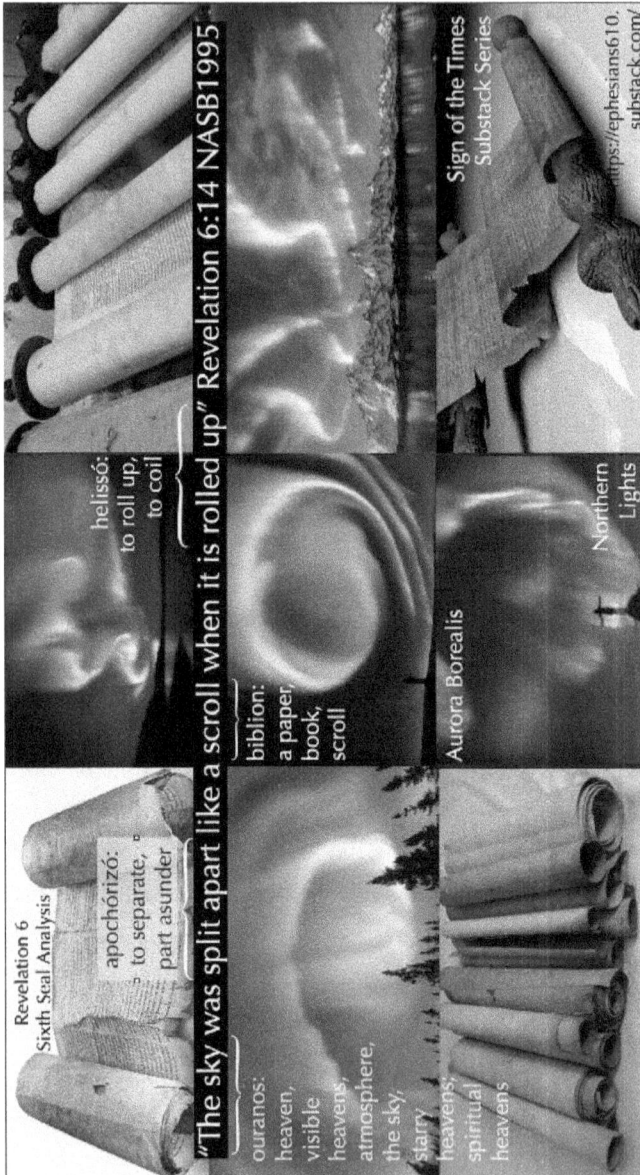

12.3 Hypothesis: Revelation 6:14a describes the Aurora Borealis

Interpretation: Revelation 6:14a, refers to the northern lights or aurora borealis which aligns itself well in context to the prophecy in Luke that you will see signs in the sun, moon, and stars.

External evidence: The increasing sightings of northern lights are in temporal proximity to the Earthquake of 2023, solar eclipse of 2024, blood moons of 2025, and Draconids of 2025.

12.4 What Causes Northern Lights?

The aurora borealis or northern lights are caused by charged solar particles colliding with atoms and molecules in the Earth's atmosphere, creating the light we experience as the northern lights. Here are two theories behind the Northern Lights:

- The scientific theory from man is that particularly powerful solar winds cause powerful northern lights when the direction of the solar wind is aimed at Earth.[163] The sun ejects a continuous stream of charged particles, electrons and protons, known as solar wind. There are areas on the sun where the solar magnetic field extends into the firmament.

- The Biblical Cosmology theory is that the Northern Lights are the magnetic energy from the north pole, which interacts with the firmament and the base of God's throne directly above the north pole in the Heavens.

12.5 Comets, Solar Flares, Sunspots, and CMEs

Let's review the following data points from Chapter 2 which correlated comets and earthquakes.

---

[163] https://www.visittromso.no/northern-lights/what-causes-the-northern-lights

Father Jerome Sixtus Ricard of the observatory of Santa Clara College stated,

> Therefore, planets and sunspots are indissolubly [in a way that is impossible to take apart or bring to an end, or that exists for a very long time] connected.
>
> Halley's Comet may be viewed and ranked as a formative planet. Therefore, it must have a reactive influence on the sun and consequently on the weather.[164]

Father Ricard associated increasing sunspot activity with an incoming comet which also increased the possibility of coronal mass ejections (CMEs). CMEs that are Earth-facing increase the chances of seeing Aurora Borealis and the possibility of seismic activity (to be analyzed in detail later in this book).

In addition, there are solar flares at regular intervals, which release large quantities of energy from the sun. Such flares occur in active regions around **sunspots**. Solar flares can provide very powerful outbreaks of the northern lights. Hunters of Northern lights look particularly for one type of solar flare, which is called a coronal mass ejection (or **CME**). This can create a geomagnetic storm that results in powerful northern lights even at lower latitudes.

12.6 Space Weather Reports on April 25th, 2023

> **ANOTHER CME IS COMING:** But this one will not cause a severe geomagnetic storm. Unlike the CME that struck Earth on March 23rd--a direct hit--the next CME will deliver only a glancing blow. It was hurled into space on April 24th by an explosion in the sun's southern hemisphere. Minor G1-class geomagnetic storms are possible on **April 27th** when the CME arrives.

---

[164] https://www.newspapers.com/article/los-angeles-herald-comets-tail-split/21987990/

HOW LOW DID THE NORTHERN LIGHTS GO? A CME hit Earth's magnetic field on April 23rd, a direct hit that sparked a severe G4-class geomagnetic storm. Northern lights spilled out of the Arctic Circle all the way down to the US-Mexico border (+29.5N):[165]

Fig. 12.6.1 SpaceWeather Northern Lights in Southern TX

(source: SpaceWeather.com, photo credit Brad Dwight)

"I was out shooting the night sky in the Big Bend region of Texas when I saw the alerts of the severe geomagnetic storm," says photographer Brad Dwight. "I decided to point my camera north just to see if I could see anything. These pillars exploded into view."[166]

12.7 The Sun's 11-Year Cycle

Eos, the award winning science news magazine reports, "Hearing the Sun Tock", by Russell, Jian, and Luhmann,

---

[165] https://spaceweather.com/

[166] https://spaceweather.com/

The appearance of sunspots—their number, duration, and location—suggests that the dynamics of the Sun's outer layer is synchronized with an internal clock.

Fig. 12.7.1 EOS Solar Cycle

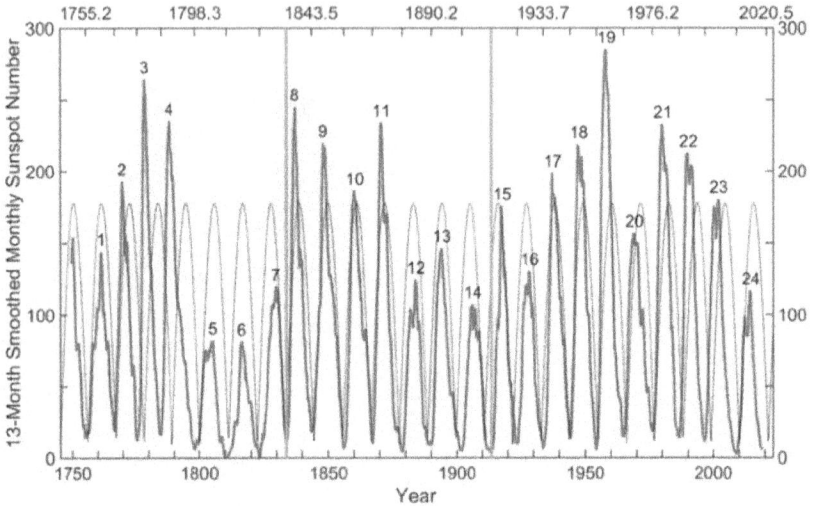

The red line shows the number of sunspots recorded annually since 1749. The dotted black line shows a 11.05-year cycle with an amplitude of 178.7, which are average measures for this series. Credit: Russell et al. (2019). Figure 6

(source EOS)

The red [solid] line shows the number of sunspots recorded annually since 1749. The dotted black line shows a 11.05-year cycle with an amplitude of 178.7, which are average measures for this series.[167]

12.8 Solar Cycle 25

K. Cartier, reports on August 2022,

The current solar cycle, number 25, started in 2019, which means that the Sun has been slowly ramping up its sunspot and flare activity for the past few years. Solar maximum, when

---

[167] https://eos.org/editors-vox/hearing-the-sun-tock

the **Sun's magnetic polarity flips** and it's expected to be the most active, is anticipated to happen sometime between **2023 and 2026**.[168]

Scientists hope that cycle 25 will continue to provide more excitement than did cycle 24—they want to see **spots and flares of all sizes and intensities and many coronal mass ejections (CMEs) that traverse interplanetary space to interact with planets' magnetic fields.**[169]

Fig. 12.8.1 Solar Cycle through 2025

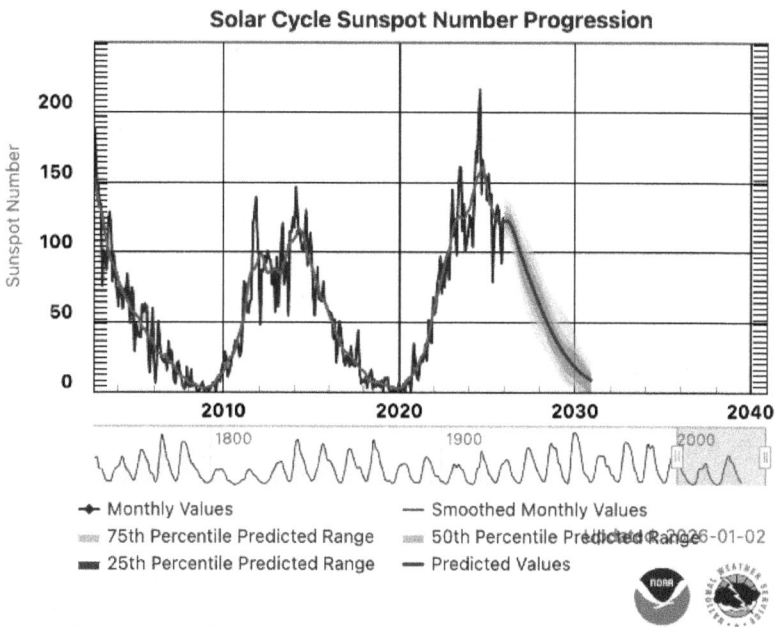

Solar Cycle Sunspot Number Progression

(Source: NOAA)[170]

In the first version of this book published in 2023, one could only estimate the number of sunspots in 2025. Now looking back on 2025, the

---

[168] https://eos.org/features/11-discoveries-awaiting-us-at-solar-max

[169] https://eos.org/features/11-discoveries-awaiting-us-at-solar-max

[170] https://www.swpc.noaa.gov/content/space-weather-enthusiasts-dashboard

results have exceeded expectations by ~40%. In Fig 12.8.1 the Solar Cycle Sunspot Number Progression shows a significant unexpected spike to ~216 sunspots, far above the projected ~155 maximum. This increase in solar activity resulted in a significant number of sightings of the Aurora Borealis.

As the solar maximum increased in cycle 25, sun spots and flares increased causing CME's that were Earth bound.

> The Northern Lights appear as undulating curtains or ribbons of light, which vary in shape, color and strength. The color of the northern lights can vary from dark blue via green and yellow to red and orange.[171]

> The altitude of the Northern Lights range from 80 to 250 km above the ground, and on rare occasions as high as 500-800 km. The average height of the Northern Lights with maximum intensity is 110-200 km, but this varies depending on the form. As the Northern Lights are well above any weather phenomenon, consequently the weather also plays an important role in seeing the Northern Lights.[172,173]

12.9 In Closing

God's omnipotent context: These are astronomical and geological signs only controlled through our God almighty, thus a perfect way for God to get the attention of the world to look up and prepare: earthquakes, solar eclipses, blood moons, meteor showers, comets, and the northern lights.

Note the timeline has been simplified to focus in on the Revelation 6 Sixth Seal signs by associating each sign to the verse. The Revelation 12 sign has been included as a time marker.

---

[171] https://www.visittromso.no/northern-lights/what-causes-the-northern-lights

[172] https://www.visittromso.no/northern-lights/what-causes-the-northern-lights

[173] https://www.wsls.com/weather/2022/03/30/aurora-borealis-to-be-visible-in-the-us-after-strong-geomagnetic-storm/

Fig. 12.10.1 Signs of the Times Revelation 6 Timeline

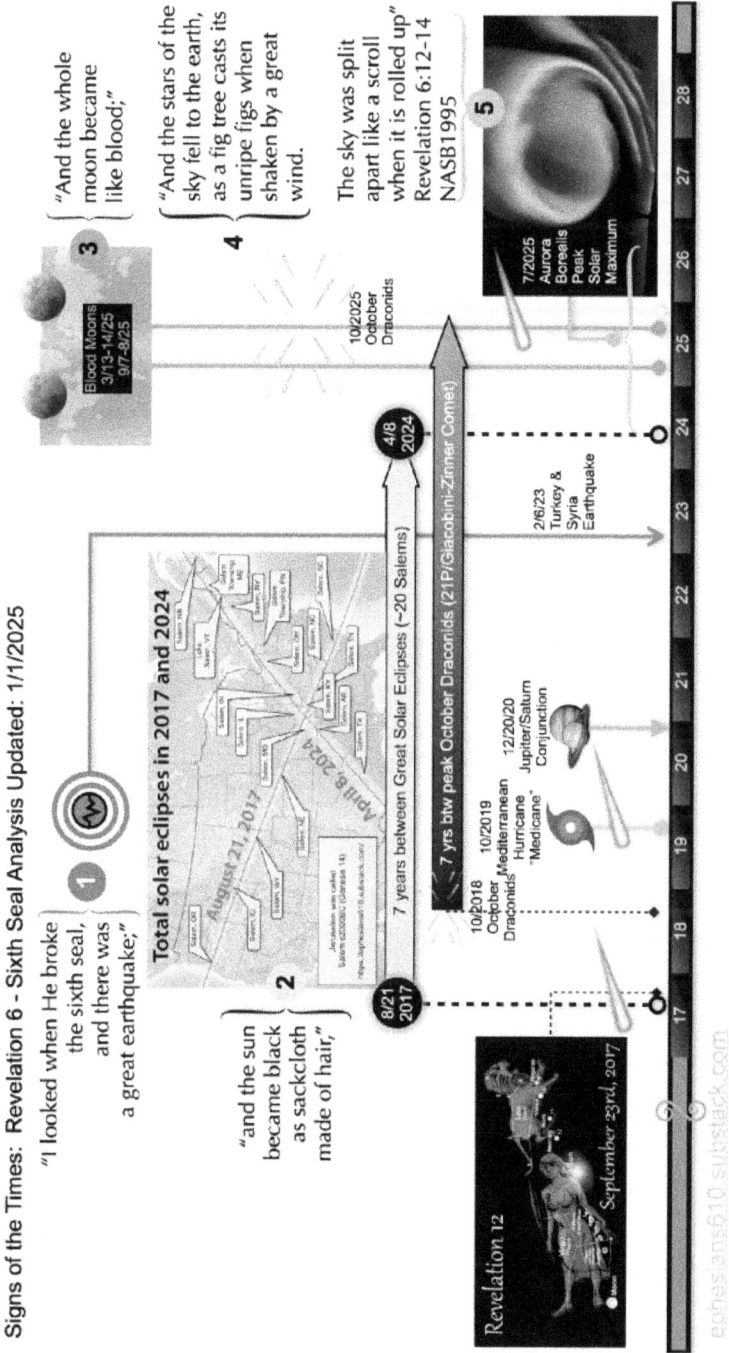

Signs of the Times: Revelation 6 - Sixth Seal Analysis Updated: 1/1/2025

1 "I looked when He broke the sixth seal, and there was a great earthquake;"

2 "and the sun became black as sackcloth made of hair,"

3 "And the whole moon became like blood;"

4 "And the stars of the sky fell to the earth, as a fig tree casts its unripe figs when shaken by a great wind."

5 The sky was split apart like a scroll when it is rolled up" Revelation 6:12-14 NASB1995

Total solar eclipses in 2017 and 2024

August 21 2017
April 8, 2024

Jerusalem was called Salem (2000BC) (Genesis 14)
https://ephesians610.substack.com/

Blood Moons 3/13-14/25 9/7-8/25

10/2025 October Draconids

7/2025 Aurora Borealis Peak Solar Maximum

7 yrs btw peak October Draconids (21P/Giacobini-Zinner Comet)

7 years between Great Solar Eclipses (~20 Salems)

10/2018 October Draconids

10/2019 Mediterranean Hurricane "Medicane"

12/20/20 Jupiter/Saturn Conjunction

2/6/23 Turkey & Syria Earthquake

4/8 2024

8/21 2017

Revelation 12
September 23rd, 2017

17 18 19 20 21 22 23 24 25 26 27 28

Chapter 13. Probability & Poetry of the Northern Lights

"The sky was split apart like a scroll when it is rolled up..."

"long quivering gold knives of light shooting up, cutting the sky..."

"would roll across the hollow of the high Heavens,
flick like a flag,
and disappear"

(source: Apostle John, W.J. Smith, and R. Kipling)

13.1 Northern Lights by W. J. Smith

William Jay Smith, wrote over 50 books of poetry and lectured at Columbia University, Oxford, and Virginia. He served on the Vermont House of Representatives from 1960 to 1962 and lived in Massachusetts and Paris, France until his death in 2015.[174]

He captures the Northern Lights in the following poem:

NORTHERN LIGHTS

I

I stepped out here on the mountainside, and saw the northern lights, cold-clear, clear-white, blue-green, long quivering gold knives of light shooting up, cutting the sky the horizon round.

Up from the valley mist rose in waves, shot up steady puffs, clear-cold in the light,

_____

[174] https://www.poetryfoundation.org/poets/william-jay-smith

And in places all the sky seemed made of moving skeins of white hair rising water-clear, stars tangled in the flowing strands.

The brook ran below (it was August, but cold); and I could hear its chill, pebbled water bubbling down, close in upon my ear.

Crickety night sounds: black trees came spangled forth, while behind a moving green gold turned them into shaggy hulks heaving in waves of light.

Trees stood, but moved, bearded and blowing, but no wind blew, and the dark itself moved, kept moving with light.

II

Mist, held deep in the valley in layers chalk-white, sheet-white, hung billowing between rock walls;

And still it rose, shade becoming light, light, shade, and as I stepped into the field, grass also moved, brightened by all these waves of hairy light.

The mountain pool caught, and tried to hold, patches of moving light, and the water, coming down from the mountain, rang swinging clear

Over evergreens overgrown; ribbons of willow, beside or behind or above the pool, leaned, moved, kept clear-turning until the whole sky moved; and I stepped into an ever-deepening river of grass, green-moving and slow, glowworm-light expanding and wavering.

Thin blades of green cut through blue-green, or green upon white, white upon gray, green upon mist-yellow, green and primrose yellow.

And primroses beside the rockpool, chill yellow in the moving mist; and light kept coming by while I moved with light moving, stood (leapt), reached (held) Earth-air (whole-part), clear-cold and all white.

(source: American Academy of Arts and Letters, William Jay Smith, 1918-2015)[175]

The beautiful words used in the poem above provide the visuals that cannot be captured in a photograph or a video. "Gold knives light… cutting the sky.. ribbons of willow, clear-turning, the whole sky moved, glowworm-light expanding and wavering… blades of green cut through blue-green…". A writer or poet would be pushed to the limit on how to describe the Northern Lights. Like Mr. Smith, Apostle John may be seeing and describing the same astronomical phenomenon:

> **14** The sky was split apart like a scroll when it is rolled up…
> *Revelation 6:14a, NASB1995*

We cannot be 100% certain that Revelation 6:14a refers to the Northern Lights. This is just an educated guess based upon the astronomical and geological signs that have been analyzed for the Sixth Seal. The timing is also intriguing as the Sun's Solar Maximum is perfectly peaking in 2025 which leads to a sun polar flip, sunspots, solar winds, coronal mass ejections (CMEs)… that may hit the Earth's protective magnetosphere, which cause the Aurora Borealis known as the Northern Lights.

13.2 Solar Cycle 25

Solar cycles repeat every ~11 years:

> The current cycle, the 25th since records began in 1755, kicked off in 2019 and, according to official predictions, was supposed to be extremely mild, peaking with about 115 monthly sunspots in 2025. The solar cycle is the **approximately 11-year ebb and flow** in the sun's magnetic activity that manifests in the number of sunspots, solar flares and eruptions. These cycles vary in intensity, with

---

[175] https://artsandletters.org/tribute/william-jay-smith/

the weakest on record having produced less than a hundred spots per month during the maximum and the strongest peaking with nearly 300. [176]

Solar Cycle 25 is predicted to continue until 2030, with peak sunspot activity expected in 2025, according to the NASA/NOAA panel of solar science expert.[177]

The Sun is now in Solar Cycle 25, which is heating up more than experts predicted! [Sunspots are at a] **9-year** high![178]

Published April 20, 2023, Tereza Pultarova, reports on Space.com, Solar activity may peak 1 year earlier than thought [in 2024 vs 2025].[179]

Northern Lights and Solar Maximum Peaks

1 out of 11 years = 1 / 11

From the previous sign:

The comet 21P/Giacobini-Zinner rotates the sun every 6.62 years.

Probability of the 21P/G-Z comet and Solar Maximum are in the same year is: 1/(6.62 x 11) = 1/72.82

The above is relatively rare at one out of 72.82, however, if we combine the one in 11 years Solar Maximum cycle with all the signs of Revelation 6, the Sixth Seal:

Probability of the Turkey earthquakes, two solar eclipses, two total lunar eclipses in 2025, a meteor shower (not including the probability of the comets), and an increase in northern lights. = 1/(1.7603904e+13 x 11) = 1/1.9364294e+14

= one in one hundred ninety-three trillion six hundred forty-two billion nine hundred forty million

---

[176] https://www.space.com/sun-solar-maximum-may-arrive-early

[177] https://www.almanac.com/solar-cycle-25-sun-heating

[178] https://www.almanac.com/solar-cycle-25-sun-heating

[179] https://www.space.com/sun-solar-maximum-may-arrive-early

= 5.1641439e-15

This clearly reaches the supernatural unseen realm of impossibility where only God can make this possible.

Below are two additional literary examples describing these lights of the high Heavens.

13.3 The Second Jungle Book by R. Kipling

"The sky above them was an intense velvety black,
changing to bands of Indian red on the horizon,
where the great stars burned like street-lamps.

From time to time a greenish wave of the Northern Lights
would roll across the hollow of the high Heavens,
flick like a flag,
and disappear;

or a meteor would crackle from darkness to darkness,
trailing a shower of sparks behind.
Then they could see the ridged and furrowed surface
of the floe tipped and laced with strange colors
– red, copper, and bluish;
but in the ordinary starlight,
everything turned to one frost-bitten gray."
– Rudyard Kipling

(source: Rudyard Kipling, "Quiquern" in *The Second Jungle Book*.)[180]

---

[180] https://www.kiplingsociety.co.uk/quotation/quotes_quiquern-htm.htm

13.4 The Aurora Borealis by David Vedder (1790-1854)

The winter night is dark and drear,
No cheerful moon nor stars appear;
The scowling clouds are trailing on
To "sift their snows" o'er the arctic zone.
No sound is heard save the brawling din
Of shallow streamlet and mountain-linn;
Or the voice of the gale, now high, now low,
Tossing the heather to and fro,
Shaking the rushes and lady-fern
That grow round the buried warrior's cairn,
And seem like spectres to the eye
Of credulous fatuity.

In the cleft of a rugged, rifted rock,
Split by the howling thunder's shock,
An helpless Covenanter lay,
Who, fled from Bothwell's bloody fray,
Both wished and feared the coming day.
His war-worn limbs and aching head
Were wrapped in a damp and tattered plaid,
And famine, gaunt and grim, was there,
Ghastfully hovering o'er his lair;
And the brumal blast grew deadly chill,
And the night waxed darker, drearier still.
Horror, alas! had banished sleep,
He sobbed and moaned, but could not weep.

When in the twinkling of an eye,
From palpable obscurity
Tumultuous streams of glory gushed,
Ten thousand thousand rainbows rushed
And revelled through the boundless sky,
In jousting, flashing radiancy.

The Sixth Seal Signs

Careering around the welkin's brim
Like bright embattled Seraphim;
Or soaring up to the dome of Night,
Flooding the Milky-way with light;
Or streaming down on the mountain peaks,
On the muirland wastes, and the heather brakes;
On lake and river, on tower and tree,
Showering a sky-born galaxy,
Like a storm of pearls and diamonds driven,
Imbued with the gorgeous hues of Heaven!

The persecuted arose from his lair,
And poured forth his soul in praise and prayer;
His faith waxed strong, and his hope grew high,
As he upward gazed with intensity
On the lambent flames that blazed around,
And he deemed that he stood on holy ground!

"What mind," he said, "can conceive aright
The floods of uncreated light,
Which from eternity hath shone
Around the Everlasting's throne,
When such refulgent glories glow
Upon his footstool here below!"

(source: <u>David Vedder</u>)[181]

---

[181] https://poems.one/poem/david-vedder-the-aurora-borealis

Chapter 14. The Perfect Solar Storm - A Global Event

What would happen if there was a "Perfect Solar Storm"?

In today's modern high-technology world of mobile phones, tablets, laptops, smart sensors, smart power meters, smart power stations, smart cars, auto-drivers, auto-pilots, Global Positioning Systems (GPS), financial systems, healthcare systems, and Internet of Things/Bodies (IoT/IoB), mankind is extremely dependent upon telecommunication networks, applications, and appliances which all can be disrupted (i.e.: "electronically zapped") by space weather, especially by a perfect solar storm.

> Extreme space-weather events — intense solar and geomagnetic storms — have occurred in the past: most recently in 1859, 1921 and 1989. So scientists expect that, sooner or later, another extremely intense space weather event will strike Earth again. Such storms have the potential to cause widespread interference with and damage to technological systems. A National Academy of Sciences study projects that an extreme space-weather event could end up costing the American economy more than $1 trillion.[182]

Critical infrastructure such as cell towers, broadband hubs, switches, multiplexers, network time servers, gateways, etc. are often taken for granted. These critical infrastructure appliances fill our data centers, our cities, our nation-states, and link Big Tech, Big Pharma, and global governments. Our communications, transportation, automation,

---

[182] https://www.Earthmagazine.org/article/comment-weathering-perfect-storm-space/

surveillance, cloud computing, machine learning, Artificial Intelligence, and defense is reliant upon our fleet of satellites and a global mesh network,

> ...a recent paper estimates potential damage to the 900-plus satellites currently in orbit could cost between $30 billion and $70 billion. The best solution, they say: have a pipeline of comsats [communication satellites] ready for launch.[183]

14.1 A Global Phenomenon

Imagine the Aurora Borealis visible **over the majority of the globe**.... Up until this point we have been looking at an increasing number of sunspots, solar winds, and corona mass ejections (CMEs) due to the 2025 Solar Maximum, however is there a historical record of a **global event where the majority of the Earth witnessed the phenomenon?**

Yes: The Carrington Event - September 1st, 1859, Was it the largest recorded solar storm? Could it have resulted in a global Aurora Borealis phenomenon and damaged telegraph systems throughout the world, visible as far south as Cuba and Hawaii. The Carrington Event knocked out the telegraph systems around the world.

What are the odds of another Carrington Event in the near future? Answer: 10% or greater

Hypothesis: Could planetary alignments or comets influence the sunspots that could lead to a Carrington-level CME?

Answer: There was a planetary alignment on September 1st, 1859 discovered in Stellarium. However new research postulates that there may also have been a comet that caused the Carrington Event. This comet theory has been added in revised book.

---

[183] https://science.nasa.gov/science-news/science-at-nasa/2008/06may_carringtonflare

14.2 Probability of a Perfect Solar Storm

The following 2012 article was published in *Wired Magazine* referencing research by space physicist, Pete Riley,

Fig. 14.2.1 A 1 in 8 Chance of a Solar Mega-Storm

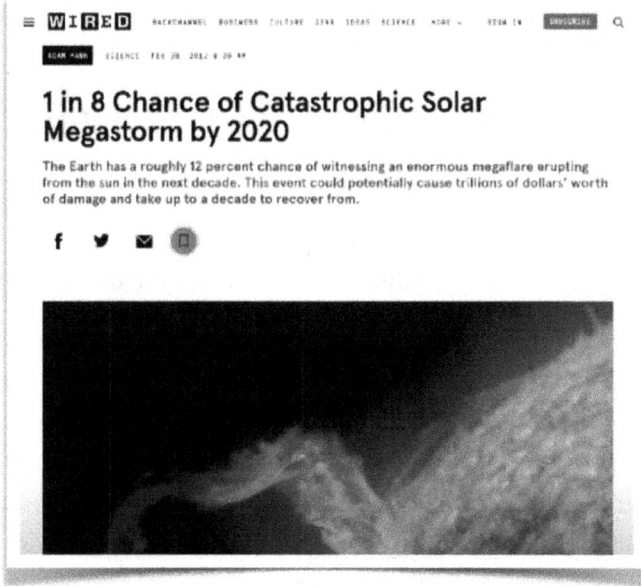

(Source: Wired)[184]

The Earth has a roughly 12 percent chance of experiencing an enormous mega-flare erupting from the sun in the next decade. **This event could potentially cause trillions of dollars' worth of damage and take up to a decade to recover from**.

Such an extreme event is considered to be relatively rare. The last gigantic solar storm, known as the Carrington Event, occurred more than 150 years ago and was the most powerful such event in recorded history.

---

[184] https://www.wired.com/2012/02/massive-solar-flare/

That a rival to this event might have a **greater than 10 percent chance of happening in the next 10 years** was surprising to space physicist Pete Riley, senior scientist at Predictive Science in San Diego, California, who published the estimate.[185]

Make note this was published in 2012. So the Earth is overdue for a major solar storm.

14.3 What happened during the Carrington Event of 1859?

At the time of the Carrington event, astronomers did not know that a CME caused the Aurora Borealis. NASA describes the morning of the event,

> At 11:18 AM on the cloudless morning of Thursday, September 1, 1859, 33-year-old Richard Carrington—widely acknowledged to be one of England's foremost solar astronomers—was in his well-appointed private observatory. Just as usual on every sunny day, his telescope was projecting an 11-inch-wide image of the sun on a screen, and Carrington skillfully drew the sunspots he saw.[186]

Note below the sunspot that Carrington drew in 1859 and also note the size of an example sunspot from 2014 in relation to Jupiter and the Earth.

As Richard Carrington was studying the sunspots, he was nearly blinded by the solar flare that exploded from the sun and resulted in a direct-hit Earth-facing CME.

> On the morning of 1 September 1859, as Richard C. Carrington was observing sunspots on the solar disk, a particularly large and complex active region destabilized,

---

[185] https://www.wired.com/2012/02/massive-solar-flare/

[186] https://science.nasa.gov/science-news/science-at-nasa/2008/06may_carringtonflare

launching an extremely fast coronal mass ejection toward Earth. A large solar flare ensued, its optical brightness lasting some 5 min and equaling that of the background Sun...

The ejecta propagated rapidly away from the Sun, generating a fast-mode wave ahead of it, which rapidly steepened into a fast-mode forward shock. The shock, traveling in excess of 2000 km s⁻¹ [***Cliver et al., 1990***] accelerated suprathermal ions in the ambient solar wind to high energies.

Fig. 14.3.1 Carrington Event Sunspot

(source: The Sun Today, and Public Domain)[187]

As these accelerated particles streamed away from the shock, they excited plasma waves that pitch angle scattered the ions, further accelerating the particles. Some of these energetic ions escaped, traveling ahead of the shock. As they streamed through the heliosphere, they amplified the ambient resonant plasma waves, simultaneously undergoing pitch angle scattering by them. Propagating through an ever-weakening magnetic field, the particles were focused and decelerated. The first particles **arrived at the Earth within an**

---

[187] https://www.thesuntoday.org/sun/surface/#sunspots

hour, although the peak intensity of the particle distribution arrived with the shock, some 17.6 h later [_Cliver and Svalgaard, 2004_].

The CME and its associated disturbance rammed into the Earth's magnetosphere, generating one of the largest magnetic storms in recorded history [_Tsurutani et al., 2003_]...

...the 1859 storm holds the record as the largest space weather event in over 400 years [**McCracken et al., 2001**]. Additionally, since the event occurred only ~150 years ago, it is a constant reminder that a similar event could reoccur any day.[188]

14.4 Testimonies of the "Sky on Fire"

When telegraphs did come back on line, many were filled with vivid accounts of the celestial light show that had been witnessed the night before. Newspapers from France to Australia featured glowing descriptions of brilliant auroras that had turned night into day.

One eyewitness account from a woman on Sullivan's Island in South Carolina ran in the Charleston Mercury:

"The eastern sky appeared of a blood red color. It seemed brightest exactly in the east, as though the full moon, or rather the sun, were about to rise. It extended almost to the zenith. The whole island was illuminated. The sea reflected the phenomenon, and no one could look at it without thinking of the passage in the Bible which says,
'the sea was turned to blood.'
The shells on the beach, reflecting light, resembled **coals of fire**."

---

[188] https://agupubs.onlinelibrary.wiley.com/doi/full/10.1029/2011SW000734

The sky was so crimson that many who saw it believed that neighboring locales were on fire. Americans in the South were particularly startled by the northern lights, which migrated so close to the equator that they were seen in Cuba and Jamaica.

Elsewhere, however, there appeared to be genuine confusion. In Abbeville, South Carolina, masons awoke and began to lay bricks at their job site until they realized the hour and returned to bed. In Bealeton, Virginia, larks were stirred from their sleep at 1 a.m. and began to warble. (Unfortunately for them, a conductor on the Orange & Alexandria Railroad was also awake and shot three of them dead.) In cities across America, people stood in the streets and gazed up at the Heavenly pyrotechnics. In Boston, some even caught up on their reading, taking advantage of the celestial fire to peruse the local newspapers.[189]

Some thought it was the end of the world, others continued with their daily activities, but Richard Carrington saw that the Heavenly pyrotechnics were triggered by the solar explosion. But what caused the explosion?

14.5 Hypothesis: A Comet & Carrington Event

In the original version of this book in 2023, it was hypothesized that planetary alignments caused the solar activity. This alignment assumes a heliocentric solar system.

After an in-depth study of Biblical Cosmology and an analysis of comets, this book also includes the following research which proposes that a comet split and fragments may have interacted with the sun and/or Earth to trigger a CME, auroras, magnetic storm, and seismic activity.

---

[189] https://www.history.com/news/a-perfect-solar-superstorm-the-1859-carrington-event

In September 2024, Boris R. German, published the following research paper, "The 1859 Carrington event, 3D/Biela comet and solar white-light flares".[190] The paper builds a case with the following observations,

> The Carrington event's exceptionally solar genesis also faces unresolved problems of abnormal brightness, color, and locality (e.g., in Salvador and Chile) of the low-latitude auroras [Hayakawa, 2018].

> On the same days, earthquakes were recorded in El Salvador [Ribeiro, 2011], which is inexplicable by the activity of the Sun.

> Since, on the day of the maximum of the Andromedids meteor shower in 1885 found the Mazapil iron meteorite [Hidden, 1887], the 3D/Biela comet could have magnetic fragments. The movement of magnetized Andromedids meteors particles along the magnetic geofield lines would have produced effects indistinguishable from solar disturbations, including induction telluric currents. In this case, it is excessive to postulate *CMEs*.

German concludes that the Carrington Event was less likely a CME and possibly caused by a Comet Biela (3D/Biela), which has ceased to exist. If this hypothesis is true he postulates that there may not have been a CME. However, given the earlier research by Father Ricard, where comets can interact with the sun, it potentially may have been the perfect storm where Comet Biela increased solar activity to cause the sun spots, CME, subsequent earthquakes, and low-latitude auroras. Let's take a closer look at 3D/Biela.

14.6 Comet 3D/Biela

Jenniskens, P and Vaubaillon, J. published in 2007, "3D/Biela and the Andromedids: Fragmenting versus Sublimating Comets"

---

[190] German, B. R. (2024). The 1859 Carrington event, 3D/Biela comet and solar white-light flares. https://www.researchgate.net/publication/382659606_The_1859_Carrington_event_3DBiela_comet_and_solar_white-light_flares

Fig. 14.6.1 Comet 3D/Biela - Parts A & B

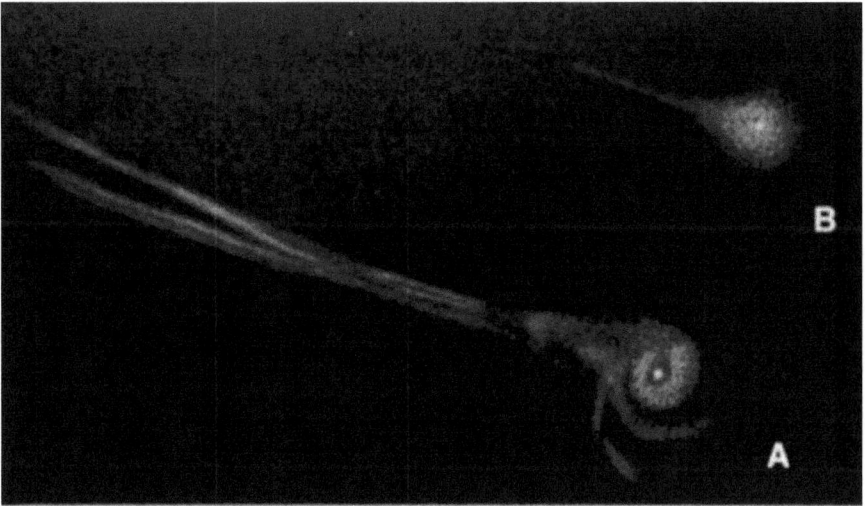

Comet 3D/Biela broke up in 1842/1843 and continued to disintegrate in the returns of 1846 and 1852. When meteor storms were observed in November of 1872 and 1885, it was surmised that those showers were the debris from that breakup.

This could have come from one of two sources: (1) the initial separation of fragments near aphelion or (2) the continued disintegration of the fragments afterward. Alternatively, the meteoroids could simply have come from water vapor drag when the fragments approached perihelion (option 3). We investigated the source of the Andromedid storms by calculating the dynamical evolution of dust ejected in a normal manner by water vapor drag in the returns from 1703 to 1866, assuming that the comet would have remained similarly active over each return. In addition, we simulated the isotropic ejection of dust during the initial fragmentation event at aphelion in December of 1842. We conclude that option 2 is the most likely source of meteoroids encountered during the 1872 and 1885 storms, but this accounts for only a relatively small amount of mass lost in a typical comet breakup.[191]

So here we have a possible explanation of a comet that splits and disintegrates leaving a dust path of particles that potentially interacted with the sun and Earth in a way that triggered a series of events observed by witnesses of the Carrington Event. Could this be something that occurs again?

14.7 Giant Sunspots in 2025

On December 5th, 2025, Harry Baker reported in livescience.com a "Giant sunspot on par with the one that birthed the Carrington Event has appeared on the sun — and it's pointed right at Earth"

> A massive new sunspot complex, dubbed AR 4294-4296, has emerged on the sun and is facing directly at Earth. The dark patch is on par with the infamous sunspot that birthed the 1859 Carrington Event — but, for now, it's staying quiet.[192]

Fortunately no large CMEs resulted from these sunspots but it was a reminder of what was experienced in 1859. Maybe the ingredients were not exactly right yet and God will be reserving a future event for the Earth.

14.8 In Closing

This Sixth Seal is a series of astronomical and geological signs that have been given to Apostle John by Jesus to document for future generations. These signs all potentially point to God's astronomical clock within the Fig Tree generational time markers.

---

[191] Jenniskens, P., Vaubaillon J. (2007). 3D/Biela and the Andromedids: Fragmenting versus Sublimating Comets. https://ui.adsabs.harvard.edu/abs/2007AJ....134.1037J/abstract

[192] Baker, H. (2025). Giant sunspot on par with the one that birthed the Carrington Event has appeared on the sun — and it's pointed right at Earth. LiveScience.com. https://www.livescience.com/space/the-sun/giant-sunspot-on-par-with-the-one-that-birthed-the-carrington-event-has-appeared-on-the-sun-and-its-pointed-right-at-earth

If God really wanted to destroy our hand-held idols and halt the globalist attempt for Transhumanism with track and trace surveillance under the skin, what better way then an Earth-facing perfect CME exploding from our sun, penetrating our magnetosphere, splitting the skies with the awe inspiring Aurora Borealis, and globally impacting critical infrastructure with a complete blackout of communication.

Some say the blood moons are a harbinger for Israel and the total solar eclipses are a harbinger for all other nations. What if an incoming comet causes the perfect CME "great wind", and a great meteor storm where stars fall like unripe figs?

Is the Sixth Seal warning of a solar storm and its impact on mankind? Is the Sixth Seal an "Early Warning"?

The answer is for each reader to analyze on their own in prayer and study:

- Analyze each sign, those that have occurred, those that are going to occur, and those that may occur.

- Study the scripture and the science as well as the statistics.

- Review the hypothetical interpretations and look at the probability of these signs aligning with the scripture

  - Are they mathematically more than coincidence?

Personally, this study has opened my eyes to an unseen realm of omnipotence and orchestration that my mind cannot grasp. These events could not have occurred by chance.

The signs reveal God's everlasting control that He made everything. The Heavens were set into motion at the creation of the sun, moon, and stars as signs. The signs were placed there for us. God wants us to follow the commands of Jesus Christ to persevere and overcome and to look up for His redemption draws near.

Chapter 15. Solar Winds Trigger Seismic Events

A study of science, statistics, and scripture to build up the perseverance of the saints.

> ¹⁴ The sky was split apart like a scroll when it is rolled up,
> AND
> every mountain and island were moved out of their places.
> **Revelation 6:14, NASB1995**

*Aurora Borealis/Northern Lights **AND** Earthquakes/Volcanoes Are Related.*

This Sixth Seal is a series of astronomical and geological signs that have been given to Apostle John by Jesus to document for future generations. These signs all potentially point to God's astronomical clock within the Fig Tree generational time markers.

- What if the 2nd total solar eclipse in 2024 is aligned with 7 objects in our solar system including the sun?

  - Would this cause excessive solar activity in 2024?

  - **Hypothesis:** Planetary perturbations and comets may trigger solar activity and subsequent Earthquakes.

    - German noted this in his paper in the previous Chapter 14, that on the same day as the 1859 Carrington Event, that earthquakes were recorded in El Salvador.[193]

- Is the Sixth Seal an "Early Warning" of a solar storm and its impact on the Earth's core and crust?

---

[193] German, B. R. (2024). The 1859 Carrington event, 3D/Biela comet and solar white-light flares. https://www.researchgate.net/publication/382659606_The_1859_Carrington_event_3DBiela_comet_and_solar_white-light_flares

- Is there a correlation between solar activity to Earth's seismic activity?

  - **Answer: YES** - there is a very high probability that solar activity triggers Earthquakes and volcanoes.

"The probability that it's just by chance that we observe this, is very, very low — less than **1 in 100,000**."[194]

What if solar activity and planetary alignments are potential leading indicators to watch for Earthquakes and volcanoes? Let's look at a specific example in history and also review a recently released paper regarding this solar to seismic correlation based upon 20 years of data.

15.1 The 1859 eruption of Mauna Loa

In the previous article we reviewed the perfect solar storm:

Did you know that there was a notable volcanic eruption in Hawaii in 1859? Yes in 1859, a year before the 1860 solar maximum of Solar Cycle 10, in the exact same year as the largest solar CME of 1859, which caused glowing red night skies from the Aurora Borealis and telegraph machines to spark and systematically fail, there was also a 300-day 32-mile volcanic eruption in Hawaii. The United States Geological Survey (USGS) states the following,

> The 1859 eruption of Mauna Loa began in the evening of January 23... The eruption ultimately destroyed a coastal village and fishponds at Wainanali`i and Kiholo, on the west coast of the island.
>
> This eruption is notable for several reasons. It is the most voluminous eruption in the post-contact period, and it **produced a 52-km- (32-mile-) long lava flow, longest in the state. The eruption lasted for approximately 300 days,**

---

[194] https://www.astronomy.com/science/powerful-eruptions-on-the-sun-might-trigger-Earthquakes/

the second most lengthy of all Mauna Loa eruptions since the arrival of Europeans in Hawai`i...

...People reported that, during the early days of the eruption, the glow from the eruptive activity was sufficient to allow one to read newsprint in Waimea! People on the south side of Maui saw the glow from across the channel.[195]

15.2 Correlation of Solar Activity with Seismic Events

In July, 2020, M. Groh, published "Powerful eruptions on the Sun might trigger Earthquakes", *Astronomy,* where she noted that powerful Earthquakes often do not occur randomly but they occur in clusters or groups and do not have an even distribution. Because Earthquakes tend to occur in groups, scientists have suggested that there is something triggering this worldwide phenomenon.[196]

Ms. Groh cites a paper that reviewed 20 years of data and their findings show a correlation between solar activity in our sun with seismic events on Earth.

SOHO, which is located 900,000 miles (1.45 million kilometers) from Earth, keeps its sights set on the Sun, which helps scientists track how much solar material ends up striking our planet. By comparing the ISC-GEM Global Instrumental Earthquake Catalogue — a historical record of strong Earthquakes — to SOHO data, the **scientists noticed more strong Earthquakes occurred when the number and velocities of incoming solar protons increased. Specifically,**

---

[195] https://www.usgs.gov/news/volcano-watch-1859-eruption-mauna-loa-and-its-human-impact

[196] https://www.astronomy.com/science/powerful-eruptions-on-the-sun-might-trigger-Earthquakes/

when protons streaming from the Sun peaked, there was a spike in quakes above magnitude 5.6 for the next 24 hours.

"This statistical test of the hypothesis is very significant," De Natale says. "The probability that it's just by chance that we observe this, is very, very low — less than **1 in 100,000.**"

Giuseppe De Natale, is research director at the National Institute of Geophysics and Volcanology in Rome and co-author of the new study.[197]

Marchitelli, V., Harabaglia, P., Troise, C., and Natale, G. published "On the correlation between solar activity and large Earthquakes worldwide." *Sci Rep* **10**, 11495 (2020):

We found clear correlation between proton density and the occurrence of large Earthquakes ($M > 5.6$), with a time shift of one day. The significance of such correlation is very high, with probability to be wrong lower than 10^{-5}. The correlation increases with the magnitude threshold of the seismic catalogue. A tentative model explaining such a correlation is also proposed, in terms of the reverse piezoelectric effect induced by the applied electric field related to the proton density. This result opens new perspectives in seismological interpretations, as well as in Earthquake forecast.[198]

15.3 Paper's Conclusion

This paper gives the first, strongly statistically significant, evidence for a high correlation between large worldwide Earthquakes and the proton density near the magnetosphere, due to the solar wind.... Such pulses would be generated by large electrical discharges channeled in the large faults, due to their high conductivity because of

[197] Marchitelli, V., Harabaglia, P., Troise, C., and Natale, G. (2020). "On the correlation between solar activity and large Earthquakes worldwide." *Sci Rep* **10**, 11495 . https://www.nature.com/articles/s41598-020-67860-3

[198] Ibid.

fractured and water saturated fault gauge. The widespread observations of several macroscopic electro-magnetic effects before, or however associated to large Earthquakes, support our qualitative model to explain the observed, **highly statistically significant, proton density-Earthquakes correlation**.[199]

Therefore, sunspots increase during the Solar Maximum peaking in 2025. As we saw with the 1859 Carrington Event, we are overdue for another potential CME. And between 2017 to 2025, Earth observers sighted three "interstellar visitors" and at least 11 comets that churned up solar and seismic activity.

15.4 In Closing

[14] The sky was split apart like a scroll when it is rolled up, AND every mountain and island were moved out of their places.
Revelation 6:14, NASB1995

The 2020 research paper correlating proton density with large Earthquakes continues to reveal the truth in the prophetic scriptures of Revelation 6:14.

- Solar winds increase proton density in the atmosphere, which cause the Aurora Borealis (Northern Lights)
  - "The sky was split apart like a scroll when it is rolled up"
- Large worldwide Earthquakes and volcanoes
  - "Every mountain and island were moved out of their places."

---

[199] Marchitelli, V., Harabaglia, P., Troise, C., and Natale, G. (2020). "On the correlation between solar activity and large Earthquakes worldwide." *Sci Rep* **10**, 11495 . https://www.nature.com/articles/s41598-020-67860-3

Chapter 16. Prophecy and Probability Summary

> I looked when He broke the sixth seal, and
> there was a **great Earthquake**; and
> the **sun became black as sackcloth made of hair**, and
> **the whole moon became like blood**; and
> the stars of the sky fell to the Earth,
> as a fig tree casts its unripe figs when shaken by a great
> wind.
> The **sky was split apart like a scroll when it is rolled up**, and
> **every mountain and island were moved out of their places.**
> Revelation 6:12-14, NASB1995

The Sixth Seal is a series of astronomical and geological signs that have been given to Apostle John by Jesus to document for future generations.

1. **The Fig Tree Prophecy:** These unveiling signs reveal God's astronomical clock within the Fig Tree generational time markers of 2018 to 2028. The 2023 Earthquake falls right in the middle of these markers: 2018-2023-2028.

2. **God's Year « Man's Year:** As in 2nd Peter 3:8, time is not the same for man as it is for God. Thus theses signs are literally in a blink of an eye for God. Starting with the Revelation 12 sign leading up to a high concentration of signs between 2023 to 2025.

3. **The Four Horsemen:** The timeline of the sixth seal follows the Four Horsemen of Seals 1 to 4. Seal 5 covers the martyrs that have been killed. The Four Horsemen were given the authority to kill 1/4th of the world's population (i.e. depopulation).

4.   Using a Futurist interpretation of Revelation 6 the timeline leads us to the Sixth Seal and suddenly the Heavens come alive with total solar eclipses, blood moons, comets, meteor showers, Aurora Borealis, solar winds, seismic activity, and rare planetary alignments.

Upon the publication of this article in June, 2023, the timeline (included at the end of this chapter) displays actual events that have occurred or will occur. Through astronomical software like Stellarium, we have the ability to calculate the actual date and time of future total solar eclipses, total lunar eclipses, solar maximums, and comet orbits that generate meteor showers. These just so happen to align themselves with the Revelation Chapter 6 - Sixth Seal scripture references outlined in the following order.

16.1 The Sixth Seal: Sign #1 - Earthquake(s)

"[12] I looked when He broke the sixth seal, and there was a great Earthquake;"
Revelation 6:12, NASB1995[200]

In 2023 there were two Earthquakes in Turkey and on the border of Syria:

1.   February 5th, 2023 - Magnitude 7.8 Pazarcik

2.   February 6th, 2023 - Magnitude 7.5 Elbistan

The probability of these conditional events is calculated using the following formula:

1/3000 x 1/20 = 1/60,000 = **1 out of 60 thousand**

16.2 The Sixth Seal: Sign #2 - Total Solar Eclipse(s)

"and the sun became black as sackcloth *made* of hair..."

---

[200] https://www.biblegateway.com/passage/?search=Revelation+6&version=NASB1995

Revelation 6:12, NASB1995[201]

There are two total solar eclipses of significance on 2017 and 2024 which form an "X" across North America and just so happen to cross ~20 Salems with a "Cross of Peace" near the center.

The probability of these supernatural elements (i.e.: the ~20 Salems and a "Cross of Peace") have been calculated in the article which quickly reach one in $1/4.2e69$, but for a conservative estimate the calculations below only factor in the probability of a total solar eclipse using the probability of 1/400.

> 1/400 x 1/400 = 1/160,000 = 1/160k
>
> Estimated Probability of 2 Independent Total Solar Eclipses, the M7.8 Earthquake and the M7.5 Aftershock
>
> 1/60k x 1/160k = 1/9.6e9 = **1 out of 9.6 Billion**

16.3 The Sixth Seal: Sign #3 - Blood Moon(s)

> "and the whole moon became like blood;"

Revelation 6:12, NASB1995[202]

The probability of a total lunar eclipse, or blood moon, is relatively high, but it is rare to have a pair of blood moons that cover all nations with blood. The last time this happened was 1902.

> 2025 - 1902 (The last time 2 total lunar eclipses covered all nations with blood) = 123 years
>
> Probability of 2 independent total lunar eclipses is 1/(1.5 x 1.5) = 1/2.25
>
> Probability of 2 total lunar eclipses where the entire world has visibility to the whole moon turning to blood:
>
> 1/(123 x 2.25) = 1/277

---

[201] Ibid.

[202] Ibid.

Probability of the Earthquake and aftershock, two solar eclipses, and two total lunar eclipses where the whole moon became like blood for all the nations to see:

1/(9.6 Billion x 277)

=1/(2.6592e+12)

= one in two trillion six hundred fifty-nine billion two hundred million

16.4 The Sixth Seal: Sign #4 - Meteor Shower(s)

> "[13] and the stars of the sky fell to the Earth, as a fig tree casts its unripe figs when shaken by a great wind."
>
> _Revelation 6:12, NASB1995_[203]

The hypothetical interpretation of this sign is the Draconids meteor shower from the constellation Draco, the dragon of old, the serpent, representing Satan. The interesting thing is this shower has fluctuated and become a storm where it reached 10,000 to 12,000 meteors per hour in 1933 and 1946, respectively. Normally the shower hovers between 3 to a few hundred meteors per hour (i.e.: Zenith Hourly Rate (ZHR)). In the probability calculations below, we only use the orbit of the comet 21P/Giacobini-Zinner of 6.62 years.

Probability of the Earthquake and aftershock,

two solar eclipses,

two total lunar eclipses where the whole moon became like blood for all the nations to see, and

a Draconids meteor shower with a high Zenith Hourly Rate (ZHR):

= 1/(2.6592e+12 x 6.62)

= 1/1.7603904e+13

---

[203] Ibid.

= one in seventeen trillion six hundred three billion nine hundred four million

Note the <u>planetary alignment</u> discovered, which will "cook" the comet upon perihelion to increase the ZHR has not been factored into the above calculation. If the planetary alignment was factored into the calculation the probability would be 1./1.6e+18.

16.5 The Sixth Seal: Sign #5 - A. Aurora Borealis

"[14] The sky was split apart like a scroll when it is rolled up,"

Revelation 6:12, NASB1995[204]

With this sign we analyzed the science and the poetry of the beautiful Aurora Borealis or Northern Lights. To calculate the probability we use the solar cycle of 11 years where the solar winds peak during the solar maximum.

Probability of the Earthquake and aftershock,

two solar eclipses,

two total lunar eclipses where the whole moon became like blood for all the nations to see,

a meteor shower, and

an increase in northern lights due to a peak in the solar maximum

= 1/(1.7603904e+13 x 11)

= 1/1.9364294e+14

= one in one hundred ninety-three trillion six hundred forty-two billion nine hundred forty million

= 5.16e-15 which is basically zero, mathematically impossible

---

[204] Ibid.

Fig. 16.5.1 Probability Timeline

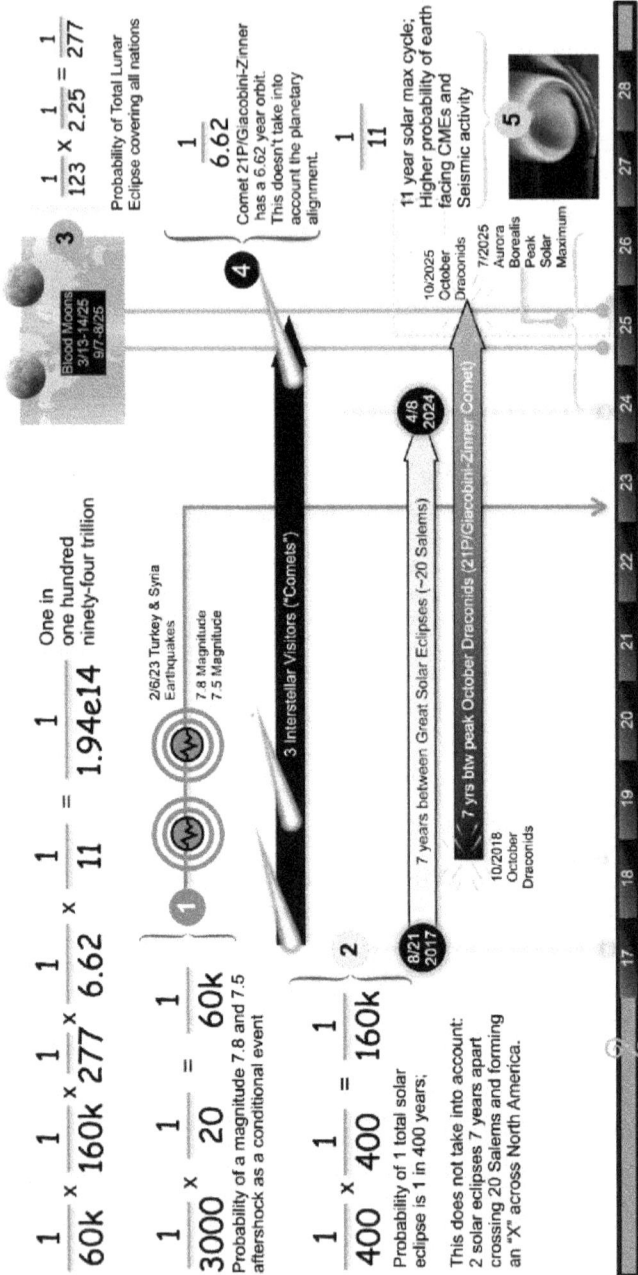

$$\frac{1}{60k} \times \frac{1}{160k} \times \frac{1}{277} \times \frac{1}{6.62} \times \frac{1}{11} = \frac{1}{1.94e14}$$ One in one hundred ninety-four trillion

$$\frac{1}{3000} \times \frac{1}{20} = \frac{1}{60k}$$

Probability of a magnitude 7.8 and 7.5 aftershock as a conditional event

$$\frac{1}{400} \times \frac{1}{400} = \frac{1}{160k}$$

Probability of 1 total solar eclipse is 1 in 400 years;

This does not take into account: 2 solar eclipses 7 years apart crossing 20 Salems and forming an "X" across North America.

2/6/23 Turkey & Syria Earthquakes
7.8 Magnitude
7.5 Magnitude

3 Interstellar Visitors ("Comets")

8/21 2017

7 years between Great Solar Eclipses (~20 Salems)

4/8 2024

7 yrs btw peak October Draconids (21P/Giacobini-Zinner Comet)

10/2018 October Draconids

$$\frac{1}{123} \times \frac{1}{2.25} = \frac{1}{277}$$

Probability of Total Lunar Eclipse covering all nations

$$\frac{1}{6.62}$$

Comet 21P/Giacobini-Zinner has a 6.62 year orbit. This doesn't take into account the planetary alignment.

$$\frac{1}{11}$$

11 year solar max cycle; Higher probability of earth facing CMEs and Seismic activity

Blood Moons
3/13-14/25
9/7-8/25

10/2025 October Draconids

7/2025 Aurora Borealis Peak Solar Maximum

1
2
3
4
5

17 18 19 20 21 22 23 24 25 26 27 28

The infographic above can be shared with those that need to see God's amazing astronomical clock in action. The odds that this was by chance is extremely rare at approximately **one in one hundred ninety-four trillion**.

In the sections below, Sign #5 was further analyzed using the 1859 Carrington Event and the probability of solar activity causing seismic activity on Earth.

16.6 The Sixth Seal: Sign #6 - B. Seismic Activity

> "and every mountain and island were moved out of their places."
> *Revelation 6:12-13, NASB1995*[205]

After the Carrington Event of 1859, scientists believe there is a 10%+ chance of a perfect solar storm, especially as the solar maximum is peaking in 2025.

Scientists compared 20 years of historical Earthquakes with solar proton density data and found that when solar proton density peaked, there was a spike in Earthquakes above Magnitude 5.6 for the next 24 hours. Therefore, the Earth may be entering a high watch period of solar storms, northern lights, earthquakes and volcanoes.

> "This statistical test of the hypothesis is very significant... The probability that it's just by chance that we observe this, is very, very low — less than **1 in 100,000**."[206]

Factoring this into the equation we get an even smaller mathematical zero which is impossible.

---

[205] Ibid.

[206] Marchitelli, V., Harabaglia, P., Troise, C., and Natale, G. (2020). "On the correlation between solar activity and large Earthquakes worldwide." *Sci Rep* **10**, 11495 . https://www.nature.com/articles/s41598-020-67860-3

Chapter 17. Updates & What's Next?

17.1 Earthquakes and Volcanoes

On August 28th, 2023, a 7.0 magnitude earthquake strikes in Bali, Indonesia below the sea.[207]

On August 8th, 2025, an 8.8 magnitude earthquake strikes near the Kamchatka Peninsula which then triggers a series of six to then seven volcanoes. Russian seismologists called this a "parade of volcanic eruptions" that had not happened for over 300 years[208]. Other eruptions and seismic activity increased along the Ring of Fire in South East Asia, Alaska, California, and Latin America.[209]

WION (World is One News, India) reports on December 7th, 2025,

> In Ethiopia, the Hayli Gubbi volcano erupted on Sunday. It sent a cloud of ash and smoke high into the air, prompting flight cancellations as hot clouds drifted toward other countries as far as India and China. The long-dormant Hayli Gubbi volcano, located in the Afar region near the Ethiopian border, erupted for the first time in nearly 12,000 years.

> ...Volcanoes, faults, and fire are rewriting the map of our planet in real time. And now, scientists say a brand new ocean is being born under our feet. A dramatic geological shift is ripping through East Africa. A tear so vast it could redraw global geography.

---

[207] https://abcnews.go.com/International/wireStory/powerful-Earthquakes-rock-indonesias-bali-java-islands-casualties-102631451

[208] https://ephesians610.substack.com/p/parade-of-volcanoes-planets-88-and#footnote-3-170545834

[209] https://www.yahoo.com/news/articles/massive-earthquake-just-caused-parade-130000334.html

Thousands of miles away, Indonesia, home to more than 100 active volcanoes, is glowing again. In the last 30 days, Indonesia recorded 1,400 quakes of magnitude up to 6.4.

The Pacific fire belt ignites. Samu rumbles. Then Sanjang API bursts. Hours later, Lewotobi joins in three eruptions in near succession. Indonesia lies in the ring of fire where 90% of the world's quakes occur due to interactions among 15 major tectonic plates.

To the north, Russia's Bizani roars, blasting ash 10 km into the air. A vast plume drifting across Kamchatka, reaching commercial airlines. Pilots are warned, flights are diverted. It's a display of raw geological power. And yet within the destruction lies beauty.[210]

17.2 Revelation 6:12-13 Caves?

The Sixth Seal in Revelation 6 concludes with a picture of men preparing for God's wrath:

> Then the kings of the Earth and the great men and
> the commanders and the rich and the strong and every slave
> and free man hid themselves in the caves and among the
> rocks of the mountains; and they said to the mountains and
> to the rocks, "Fall on us and hide us from the presence of
> Him who sits on the throne, and from the wrath of the
> Lamb; for the great day of their wrath has come, and who is
> able to stand?"
> *Revelation 6:12-13, NASB1995*[211]

---

[210] WION. (2025). Volcano ALERT LIVE: Ethiopia's Volcano Ignites Fresh Fears Of A Massive Geological Shift | WION. https://www.youtube.com/watch?v=GHScJTQCW2A&t=10237s

[211] https://www.biblegateway.com/passage/?search=Revelation+6&version=NASB1995

17.3 What picture does this paint in the modern era?

Throughout history, especially in the age of war, air raids would force men, women, and children, to take shelter into deep underground bomb shelters and caves. During natural disasters, especially tornadoes, families take shelter in underground cellars. Doomsday preppers, wealthy elites, and world governments dig deep underground shelters where they have food and the comforts of home. Deep Underground Military Bases (DUMBs) have been revealed by workers to be able to sustain life in case of a nuclear attack or some natural disaster.

However is this what John saw in his vision? The previous signs are astronomical and seismic. The degree of seismic activity where every island and mountain is moved, could cause fear in the population for them to hide, but typically an Earthquake doesn't give people enough time to hide in the mountain and caves. Furthermore, victims typically want to sleep outside during an Earthquake and not inside or underground.

Therefore, it seems more logical that they are hiding from an impending threat or danger. Something they can see coming as in the Wrath of God. Thus if we continue to read the scriptures, logically it would mean the trumpets, which are in Revelation Chapter 8.

> When the Lamb broke the seventh seal, there was silence in Heaven for about half an hour. And I saw the seven angels who stand before God, and seven trumpets were given to them.

Revelation 8:1-2, NASB1995[212]

More analysis will be required on the seven trumpets of Revelation 8. The descriptions seem to describe astronomical near Earth objects (NEO) which impact life on Earth. This research will be posted sometime in the future.

---

[212] https://www.biblegateway.com/passage/?
search=Revelation%208&version=NASB1995

Subscribe to https://ephesians610.substack.com/

17.4 How do Christians respond?

Let me leave you with some thoughts and questions to ponder:

- Do you believe the sun, moon, and stars were created for signs?

- What if the correlation of these signs reveals the truth in the prophetic scriptures of Revelation 6?

- Depending upon when you are reading this book you may ask: What if we are in the middle of the Sixth Seal Signs? Or have they occurred? Depending upon when you are reading this book you may ask: If we are in the middle of the Sixth Seal, would the Four Horsemen be riding? (See The Signs of the Four Horsemen)

- Are deaths rising? Should we fear? Should we persevere and overcome?

- How would you live your life differently?

- Does the scriptural Revelation of Jesus written by John help build your faith that we truly are in the end times?

17.5 Lift up your heads

Data and statistics can be manipulated, however, the astronomical and geological signs are self-evident and not controlled by man, but only by God.

> [25] "There will be **signs in sun and moon and stars**, and on the Earth dismay among nations, in perplexity at the roaring of the sea and the waves, [26] men fainting from fear and the expectation of the things which are coming upon the world; for the powers of the Heavens will be shaken. [27] Then they will see the Son of Man coming in a cloud with power and great glory. [28] But when these things begin to take place, straighten up and **lift up your heads, because your redemption is drawing near.**"

29 Then He told them a parable: "Behold **the fig tree** and all the trees; 30 as soon as they put forth *leaves*, you see it and know for yourselves that summer is now near. 31 So you also, when you see these things happening, recognize that the kingdom of God is near. 32 Truly I say to you, this generation will not pass away until all things take place. 33 Heaven and Earth will pass away, but My words will not pass away.

34 "**Be on guard**, so that your hearts will not be weighted down with dissipation and drunkenness and the worries of life, and **that day will not come on you suddenly like a trap**; 35 for it will come upon all those who dwell on the face of all the Earth.

36 But **keep on the alert at all times**, praying that you may have strength to escape all these things that are about to take place, and to **stand before the Son of Man**."

(**Luke 21:25-36**, NASB1995)[213]

As in Mark 13:33, Luke uses the same word, "keep on the alert at all times" in Luke 21:36, which in Greek is:

agrupneó: to be sleepless, wakeful

Usage: I am not asleep, am awake; especially: I am watchful, careful.[214]

Agrupneó is used 4 times in the Bible including Ephesians 6:18.

With all prayer and petition pray at all times in the Spirit, and with this in view, **be on the alert** with all perseverance and petition for all the saints,

Ephesians 6:18, NASB1995 [215]

---

213 https://www.biblegateway.com/passage/?search=Luke+21&version=NASB1995

214 https://biblehub.com/greek/69.htm

215 https://www.biblegateway.com/passage/?search=Ephesians+6%3A18&version=NASB1995

Epilogue

God the Orchestra Conductor

We've studied in depth the literal interpretations of the stars, solar eclipses, blood-red moons, and more. We've used the Heavens as a temperature gauge for the signs of the times.

"Imagine if the sun, moon, planets, and stars are a huge orchestra on a stage of the universe, where every instrument has a part to play in the symphony and God is the conductor.

- God has the sheet music for all players and sets the tempo and dynamics of each player.

- God knows when Jupiter and Saturn will begin their duet before Capricorn, like the trumpets and trombones playing a fanfare in the opening measures of the 1st movement.

- God knows when Jupiter plays its trumpet solo in <u>retrograde motion within the womb of Virgo</u>.

- God knows when there will be <u>meteor showers</u> in the Great Red Dragon, and God knows every single meteorite as if they are the 1st and 2nd violinists playing tremolo.

- God knows the timing of solar and lunar eclipses as solo instruments playing violin and piano cadenzas timed perfectly.

- God knows when comets appear as rare guest performances with limited seating.

- God created it all."

God perfectly placed the sun, moon, stars, and constellations (i.e.: Mazzaroth), as *signs and seasons*, far before they were corrupted by pagan gods or occult horoscopes. They were not created for worship, but we do look up as they proclaim His Glory as it is written in Psalm 19,

> The Heavens are telling of the glory of God;
> And their expanse is declaring the work of His hands.
> 2 Day to day pours forth speech,
> And night to night reveals knowledge.
> 3 There is no speech, nor are there words;
> Their voice is not heard.
> 4 Their line has gone out through all the Earth,
> And their utterances to the end of the world.
> In them He has placed a tent for the sun,
> 5 Which is as a bridegroom coming out of his chamber;
> It rejoices as a strong man to run his course.
> 6 Its rising is from one end of the Heavens,
> And its circuit to the other end of them;
> And there is nothing hidden from its heat.
> Psalm 19:1-6, NASB1995
>
> (source BibleGateway.com)[216]

The Heavens showcase His awesome creation and unfolding plan as the gears have been set in motion since the beginning of time.

Therefore let's continue to pray diligently, continue to be watchful, to be alert, being ready for His return.

Patience in Suffering

7 Be patient, therefore, brothers, until the coming of the Lord. See how the farmer waits for the precious fruit of the Earth, being patient about it, until it receives the early and the late rains. 8 You also, be patient. Establish your hearts, for the coming of the Lord is at hand. 9 Do not grumble against one

---

[216] https://www.biblegateway.com/passage/?
search=Psalm+19%3A1-6%2C&version=NASB1995

another, brothers, so that you may not be judged; behold, the Judge is standing at the door.

James 5:7–9, ESV[217]

Prayer

For those that are searching for answers, I pray that this research may help spark deeper study into God's Word. For we know in the beginning there was the *Word* (See John 1:1; Greek: *Logos*). And God created the lights in the Heavens for signs and seasons (See Genesis 1:14) to help us be alert and watchful.

If your heart has been moved and you have not accepted Jesus Christ as your Savior. Please follow Pastor JD Farag's ABC's which have been included:

ABC: Admit, Believe, and Call

ADMIT THAT YOU'RE A SINNER.

• This is where that godly sorrow leads to genuine repentance for sinning against the righteous God and there is a change of heart, we change our mind and God changes our hearts and regenerates us from the inside out.

BELIEVE IN YOUR HEART THAT JESUS CHRIST DIED FOR YOUR SINS, WAS BURIED, AND THAT GOD RAISED JESUS FROM THE DEAD.

• Believe in your heart that Jesus Christ died for your sins, was buried, and that God raised Jesus from the dead. This is trusting with all of your heart that Jesus Christ is who he said he was.

CALL UPON THE NAME OF THE LORD.

• This is trusting with all of your heart that Jesus Christ is who he said he was. Every single person who ever lived since Adam will bend their

---

[217] The Holy Bible: English Standard Version (Jas 5:7–9). (2016). Crossway Bibles.

knee and confess with their mouth that Jesus Christ is Lord, the Lord of Lords and the King of Kings.[218]

Stay focused my friends on the joy and peace that Jesus Christ brings. For God is Alpha and Omega, Beginning and the End, the First and the Last - for He is omnipotent and we look up for His soon return. He made the sun, moon, and stars for signs to those that keep watch. The Heavens proclaim His glory like a great clock in the universe.

Let's continue this journey of discovery together as we equip the saints and watch for the signs that have been unfolding before our eyes.

Ender E. Law

For more end-times watchman research in real-time:

Subscribe, Like, and Share

Join the conversation at:

https://ephesians610.substack.com

"Finally, be strong in the Lord and in his mighty power"
Ephesians 6:10, NIV

---

[218] Farag, J.D. (2022). ABC's. JD Farag. https://www.jdfarag.org/abc

About the Author

Ender E. Law is a dedicated student of Bible prophecy, a researcher of apologetics and eschatology, and the author of *The Sixth Seal Signs*, *The Covenant Signs*, *The Signs of Jonah*, and *The Signs of The Four Horsemen*. His work bridges scholarly research and biblical truth, revealing deep prophetic insights for today's generation.

Ender has led over 50 small group lectures, he holds a Certificate of Biblical Studies from the late Dr. Michael Heiser's AWKNG School of Theology where he continues his studies. With over 30 years in the high-tech industry, he holds degrees in Engineering and an MBA, bringing a unique analytical approach to biblical prophecy and end-times signs. In his younger days, he led worship for over a decade.

Through his research, writings, and speaking engagements, Ender continues to challenge, equip, and awaken believers to the urgent messages of Scripture, to strengthen their faith, to put on the Full Armor of God, and to bring nonbelievers closer to accepting Jesus Christ as their personal Savior.

He is a husband, father, and—above all—a child of God. Ender E. Law is a pseudonym

For more end-times watchman research in real-time subscribe at

https://ephesians610.substack.com

Did this book help you in some way? If so, I'd love to hear about it. Honest reviews help readers find the right book for their needs.

God Bless,

Ender E. Law